PRACTICAL JAZZ

PRACTICAL JAZZ

*A Step-by-step Guide to Harmony
and Improvisation*

by

LIONEL GRIGSON

Stainer & Bell, London

© 1988 Lionel Grigson
First published in Great Britain by
Stainer & Bell Ltd, 82 High Road, London N2 9PW

British Library Cataloguing in Publication Data
Grigson, Lionel
    Practical jazz : a step-by-step guide
    to harmony and improvisation.
    1. Jazz. Theories
    I. Title
    785.42'01

ISBN 0 85249 668 0

Printed in Great Britain by Galliard (Printers) Ltd, Great Yarmouth

CONTENTS

FOR PETE AND PAUL
(who hear it all)
and
in memory of
CHARLIE PARKER
(1920–1955)

INTRODUCTION

The purpose of harmony is to give pleasure. Pleasure is
awakened by variety of sounds. This variety is the result of
progression from one interval to another, and progression,
finally, is achieved by motion.

J. J. Fux, The Study of Counterpoint (1725)
trans. and ed. Alfred Mann
Reprinted by permission of W. W. Norton Co. Inc.

In this book I have tried to formulate a usable theory of jazz, in a way
which grows naturally out of the subject, and which at the same time is
understandable in terms of classical theory.

Part One deals with the formation and movement of the main kinds of
chord used in jazz, and their voicings in 3, 4, 5 and 6 parts. Voice-leading
principles are derived from the classical tonal sequence. The 12-bar blues
and its main variations are discussed, together with the principle of
tritone substitution.

The system of harmony described in Part One serves as a foundation
for Part Two, which deals, in an evolutionary way, with improvisation
on chord changes, starting with the blues and building up the techniques,
vocabulary and essential repertoire of bebop. The perspective is
historical, as the blues can be seen as the beginning of jazz and bebop as
the summation of the first two eras (traditional and swing) of jazz music.

This generalised view of the melodic and harmonic scope of jazz
improvisation is offered as an underpinning for today's jazz, but as an
open rather than closed system.

Lionel Grigson
Putney, 1987

PART ONE

1 INTERVALS

The effect on the ear of any chord depends on the combined effects of the intervals which make up the chord. Therefore it is essential to have a thorough knowledge of intervals both in theory and by ear: if you are asked to play an augmented 4th you should be able to do so; and if you hear this interval you should be able to name it. It is also necessary to understand the reasons for the names of intervals: a major 3rd is so called because it is the larger of the two possible 3rds which occur in the scale, and so on.

The diatonic scales on which Western music is based are sequences of two sizes of interval: tones and semitones. In jazz the two basic kinds of diatonic scale are the major scale and the minor scale:

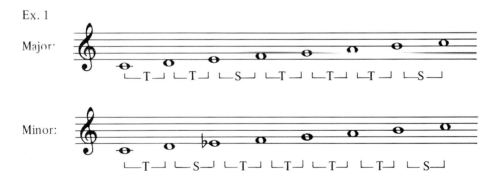

The minor scale in jazz corresponds to the ascending form of the melodic minor scale in 'classical' theory and has the same notes in its descending form (*i.e.* the 6th and 7th degrees are raised both ways).

In comparing these two kinds of diatonic scale, the only difference between them is in the intervals between their first and third notes. The major scale has the *larger* 3rd (C to E, two tones); the minor scale has the *smaller* 3rd (C to E♭, tone and semitone).

1

Simple Intervals

The intervals within a diatonic scale (major or minor) are numerically named by counting through the scale from the lower to the higher note of an interval (or from higher to lower). But because the steps of the scale are themselves of two sizes (tones and semitones), intervals with the same count can be larger or smaller by one semitone. From now on, to distinguish between larger and smaller intervals with the same scale-note count, the terms 'major' and 'minor' will be shown as 'M' and 'm':

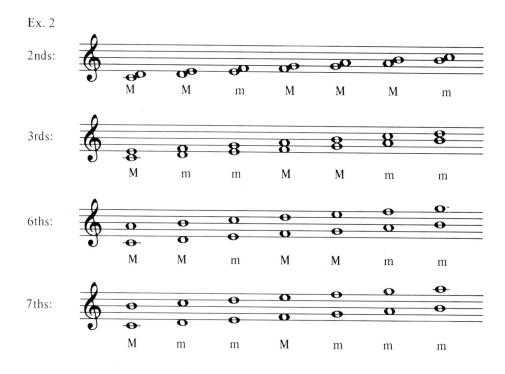

This major/minor terminology does not apply to 4ths and 5ths. The *smaller* of the two possible sizes of 4th is called 'perfect', and the larger 'augmented'. These are shown as 'P' and '+':

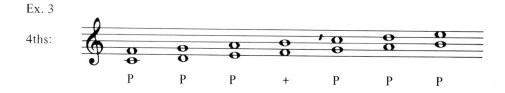

The *larger* of the two possible sizes of 5th is called 'perfect', and the smaller 'diminished'. These are shown as 'P' and '♭':

Ex. 4

5ths:

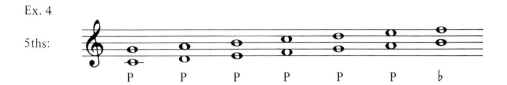

Notice that:

(i)   Perfect 4ths and 5ths are the norm (there are six of each in the major scale) and so are usually referred to simply as '4ths' and '5ths'.
(ii)   Augmented 4ths and diminished 5ths are exactly the same size, each covering three whole tones and therefore being exactly half an octave. This interval is called a 'tritone'.

Compound Intervals

So far, intervals have been less than one octave (eight notes) of the scale. These (and the octave) are called 'simple intervals'. Intervals larger than one octave are called 'compound intervals' and, as with simple intervals, they are named by the number of scale notes spanned. It is convenient to regard compound intervals as consisting of an octave plus a simple interval:

Ex. 5

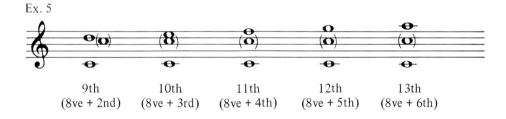

9th	10th	11th	12th	13th
(8ve + 2nd)	(8ve + 3rd)	(8ve + 4th)	(8ve + 5th)	(8ve + 6th)

Inversions of Intervals

Any simple interval (octave or less) can be 'inverted' either by raising the lower note or by lowering the higher note an octave. Each interval forms a pair with its inversion. The simplest example is:

Ex. 6

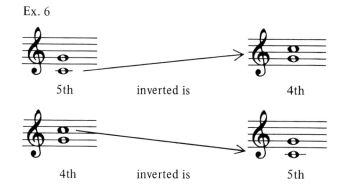

5th   inverted is   4th

4th   inverted is   5th

This table shows how inversions sound:

INTERVAL	INVERSION
Minor 2nd (Semitone)	Major 7th
Major 2nd (Tone)	Minor 7th
Minor 3rd	Major 6th
Major 3rd	Minor 6th
Perfect 4th	Perfect 5th
Augmented 4th (Tritone)	Diminished 5th (Tritone)
Diminished 5th (Tritone)	Augmented 4th (Tritone)
Perfect 5th	Perfect 4th
Minor 6th	Major 3rd
Major 6th	Minor 3rd
Minor 7th	Major 2nd (Tone)
Major 7th	Minor 2nd (Semitone)
Octave	Octave

Notice that:

(i)   Minor intervals, when inverted, become major, and vice versa.
(ii) Augmented intervals, when inverted, become diminished, and vice versa.
(iii) Perfect intervals, when inverted, remain perfect.
(iv) Tritones and octaves, when inverted, remain the same.

Consonance and Dissonance

When sounded together as a two-note chord, each interval has a distinctive quality which depends on its relative *consonance* or *dissonance*. These two terms mean roughly 'sounding together' and 'sounding in disagreement'. They refer to the relative absence or presence of interference in the frequencies of the interval. Interference between two frequencies results in 'beating' which the ear recognises as the rough or jarring effect known as 'dissonance'. The amount of dissonance in an interval depends on the ratio of its two frequencies: the simpler the ratio, the less dissonant the interval. So it is possible to arrange intervals in order of consonance to dissonance (frequency ratios in brackets):

PERFECT CONSONANCES		IMPERFECT CONSONANCES		DISSONANCES	
Unison	(1:1)	Major 3rd	(4:5)	Tone	(8:9)
Octave	(1:2)	Minor 3rd	(5:6)	Semitone	(15:16)
Fifth	(2:3)	Minor 6th	(5:8)	Minor 7th	(9:16)
Fourth	(3:4)	Major 6th	(6:10)	Major 7th	(8:15)

AMBIGUOUS
Tritone (5:7 in harmonic series)

You will see that intervals arrange themselves in opposing groups of consonances and dissonances, with an intermediate zone of imperfect consonances and the tritone (which may be dissonant or consonant according to context). These may also be seen as stable *versus* unstable intervals.

The qualities you actually do hear in intervals may have a subjective meaning (e.g. minor may sound 'sad') but there are clear differences which depend on acoustic facts. Perfect consonances can be described as pure and lacking in colour, while the imperfect consonances have a richer, warmer sound. Dissonances could be described as 'cutting' or 'jagged', particularly semitones and major 7ths; tones and minor 7ths are blunter and milder. The tritone lacks the cutting edge of the dissonances and has some of the richness of the imperfect consonances; its main quality seems to be of restlessness.

From the above table you will see that when an interval is inverted it remains in the same category of consonance or dissonance: perfect intervals remain perfect when inverted; imperfect remain imperfect and dissonances remain dissonant. This means that intervals within chords can be inverted freely without affecting the balance of consonance and dissonance within the chord. However, inversion of intervals can result in changes of intensity. The minor 2nd (semitone) loses some of its edge when inverted to a major 7th; a minor 7th is milder than a major 2nd (tone).

When intervals are compounded (spaced more than an octave apart), imperfect consonances gain depth and richness, and perfect consonances become stronger.

Tension and Relaxation

The idea of tension and relaxation is useful in relation to the movement of chords. Dissonances impart tension to a chord; perfect and imperfect consonances impart relaxation. The release of tension (dissonance) into relaxation (consonance) drives one chord to the next, as a basic principle of chord progression.

2 THE THREE MAIN CHORD TYPES

In jazz, the most used chords are 7th chords. These are four-note chords built in intervals of 3rds, so that the highest note is a 7th above the 'root'. The three lower notes of a 7th chord form a 'triad'. The middle note of a triad determines whether it is major or minor. The chord symbol for a major triad is the letter name of its 'root'; for a minor triad the root letter is followed by 'm'.

C

Cm

The three main types of 7th chord are:

(i)   Major triad + minor 7th (a '7th' chord)

C7

(ii)   Minor triad + minor 7th (a 'minor 7th' chord)

Cm7

(iii)   Major triad + major 7th (a 'major 7th' chord)

C△

The symbol △ is only used for added major 7ths; the number '7' is always used for added minor 7ths.

Exercises

(i) On the keyboard: with the right hand, construct in turn each of the three main chord types on each note of a chromatic scale ascending an octave from middle C, naming each chord as you go. Begin:

Ex. 7

(ii) Horns, guitar, bass: construct the arpeggios of each of the three main chord types on each note of the chromatic scale throughout the range of your instrument. Name each arpeggio as you go. Begin:

Ex. 8

Minimal Voicings of 7th Chords

The close-position voicings shown in examples 7 and 8, in which the notes of each chord could be no closer to each other, are really just a way of defining each chord. As melodic shapes (arpeggios), these voicings can suggest useful phrases but as chord shapes they are used rarely, if at all.

The truth of this is shown by listening to any good pianist or guitarist. Nevertheless, to see (and play) chords only as vertical blocks of stacked 3rds is all too common a fault. This vertical block approach causes two related problems:

(i) Chord sequences are seen and heard as a series of blocks in which each new chord is simply stacked up from the root. While this approach may work with many pop-type sequences it is too crude to be useful for jazz—mainly because each chord is heard as an individual entity rather than in its context as part of a logically moving progression. This in turn makes it difficult to memorise sequences of any complexity.

(ii) The principle that the dissonant notes in a chord (i.e. the 7th in a 7th chord) should normally resolve by moving by step to the next chord is ignored.

The way to avoid these problems is to apply the dual principle of **FEWEST NOTES, LEAST MOVEMENT** to chord voicing and progressions. 'Fewest notes' means that, to begin with, the only notes included in voicing the three types of 7th chord should be those necessary to identify each chord type. So the 5th can be left out because it is the same in all three types:

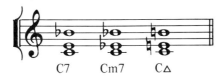

Each chord now simply consists of three notes: root, third and seventh. On the keyboard, the next step is to spread these minimal voicings by dropping the root into the bass. This gives depth and added sonority to these voicings:

Ex. 9

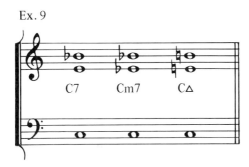

Inverting the two upper parts (3rd and 7th) produces an alternative presentation of each chord:

Ex. 10

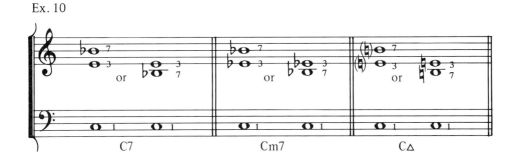

9

These three-part minimal voicings should now replace the close-position 'stacked 3rds' voicings as mental and aural images of the three types of 7th chord. On the keyboard, you should practise these alternative minimal voicings of any 7th chord without needing to refer, first, to the equivalent close-position voicing.

How to use the three 7th Chords

(i)   The major triad + minor (or 'flat') 7th is often used on the fifth of the scale (the 'dominant'). Known then as the 'dominant 7th' it usually resolves to a *major* 7th chord on the key-note (the 'tonic'):

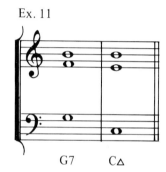

Ex. 11

         G7   C△

This 7th chord is not, however, restricted to the dominant and is often used on the tonic itself (especially in the blues).

(ii)   The minor triad + flat 7th is formed on the 2nd, 3rd and 6th degrees of the major scale. It is most often used on the second of the scale, before a dominant 7th, like this:

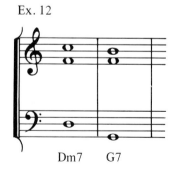

Ex. 12

      Dm7   G7

(iii) The major triad + major 7th is usually used as a tonic harmony, except in the blues.

Ex. 13

Cᴬ

Exercises

(i)   On the keyboard: with upper voices in the right hand and root in the
      left hand, construct minimal voicings of the three types of 7th chord
      on each note of a descending chromatic scale starting from C. Name
      each chord to yourself, beginning:

Ex. 14

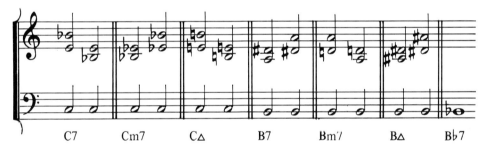

C7   Cm7   Cᴬ   B7   Bm⁷   Bᴬ   B♭7

(ii) Listening: try to find someone to play these three chord-types in
      either voicing in any order and, by ear,
      (a)   identify the type
      (b)   identify the voicing (i.e. is the 3rd or the 7th on top?)
      (c)   given the identity of a named chord as it is played, identify a
            succession of similar chords by name.

Chord Progression in Minimal Voicings

Most standard jazz chord-sequences can be reduced to minimally-
voiced progressions of the three kinds of 7th chord. Here is the sequence
to the first eight bars of *Autumn Leaves*:

| Cm7 | F7 | Bb△ | Eb△ | Am7 | D7 | Gm7 | Gm7 |

To play these harmonies on the keyboard, apply both parts of the **FEWEST NOTES, LEAST MOVEMENT** principle. Remember that inverting the upper voices of a minimal 7th chord gives two possible presentations. The first chord could look like:

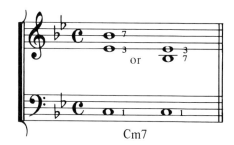

Cm7

Starting with either of these two possibilities allowed by the 'fewest notes' rule, how would you move from Cm7 to F7?

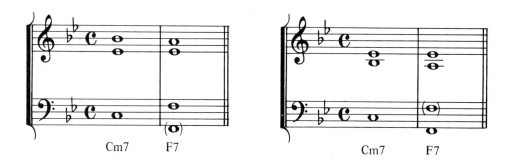

The bass may rise a 4th or fall a 5th. Which sounds better? The 7th falls a semitone to become the 3rd—and the 3rd remains where it is, to become the 7th of the second chord (i.e. 'least movement' can be no movement at all).

By following the 'least movement' rule, one upper part moves from dissonance to consonance (7 to 3) while the other does the opposite (3 to 7). As the dissonance of one upper part is resolved it reappears in the other.

Numerical Chord Description

The alphabetical chord symbols so far used in this book are the harmonic shorthand most commonly used by jazz musicians. Another useful way of describing chords replaces the letter names of chord roots with Roman numerals, to indicate the position of chords within a scale:

Scale of C major

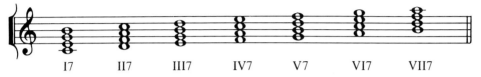

These are the 7th chords built on successive degrees of the scale of C major. In classical theory, chords described by numerals contain no notes outside the scale. In this example, chord II7 in C must be a minor 7th chord (Dm7): otherwise, it would have to include one or more accidentals.

This system has two advantages:

(i) It fixes chords in relation to a key centre.
(ii) By not referring to specific root notes by letter-name it helps to generalise chord relationships, which makes it easier to transpose sequences into different keys. For instance Dm7, G7 and C△ are chords II7, V7 and I7 in the key of C. To transpose this progression to another key it is only necessary to work out chords II7, V7 and I7 in that key.

The disadvantages are:

(i) It does not cope very well with sequences which change key.
(ii) Chords containing notes which are not in the key of the piece are hard to describe.

But by adding the jazz shorthand to classical roman numerals, these disadvantages disappear. The first eight bars of the *Autumn Leaves* sequence—in any key—becomes:

IIm7	V7	I△	IV△	VIIm7	III7	VIm7	VIm7

Apart from the fact that looking at a sequence in this way should make it easier to transpose, the main reason for introducing the numerical system is to provide an explanation of the 'II – V – I' terminology which is often used in jazz circles.

The main 'building blocks' of standard jazz chord-sequences are referred to as II – V – I or II – V progressions. That is to say, many of the chord movements which occur in such sequences are definable as II – V – I or II – V movements in different keys.

Thus, the first eight bars of *Autumn Leaves* consists of II – V – I movements in the keys of B♭ major and G minor (separated by chord IV in bar 4):

Cm7	F7	B♭△	E♭△	Am7	D7	Gm7	Gm7
II	V	I	IV	II	V	I ————	—

in B♭	in G minor

Exercise

On the keyboard, using this numerical sequence, transpose the changes into several different keys.

The Cycle of 4ths

The first eight bars of this sequence forms a 'tonal' sequence because it remains in one key-signature, even though it moves from the major to the relative minor. If, however, you take the bass line of the first four chords (which moves in perfect 4ths) and continue in perfect 4ths, you will play all twelve notes of the chromatic scale, returning to its starting point after twelve moves.

Ex. 15

II - V - I

This cycle forms a circle, moving clockwise:

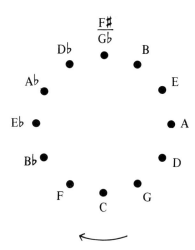

The circle also represents the order of key signatures, starting with C (no accidentals), moving clockwise and adding one flat at a time to arrive at Gb (six flats). The key of Gb is enharmonically equivalent to F♯ (six sharps), so by continuing clockwise around the circle and *omitting* one sharp at a time you will arrive back at C.

Exercises

On the keyboard, lead the following progressions through the cycle of 4ths, using the voicings indicated:

(i)   Dominant 7ths (V)

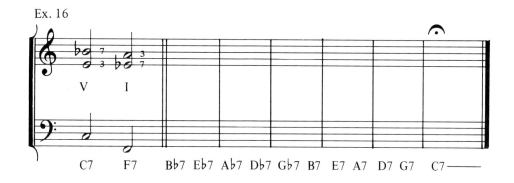

15

and

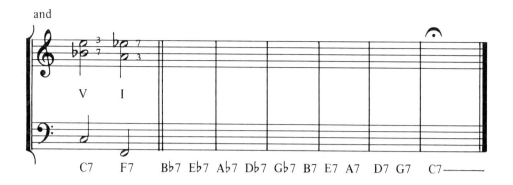

V   I

C7   F7   B♭7   E♭7   A♭7   D♭7   G♭7   B7   E7   A7   D7 G7   C7———

(ii)   Minor 7ths to dominant 7ths (II – V)

Ex. 17

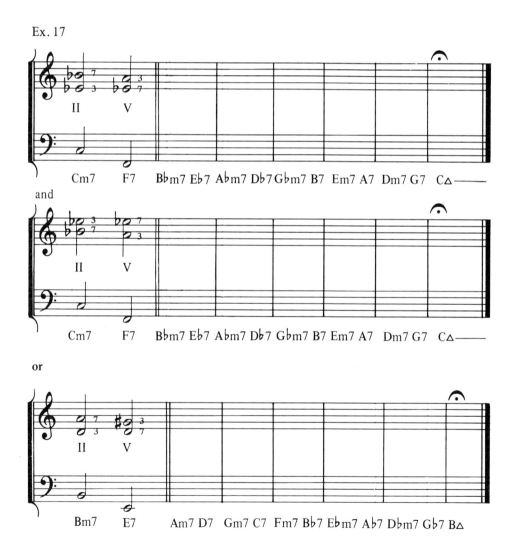

II   V

Cm7   F7   B♭m7   E♭7   A♭m7   D♭7   G♭m7   B7   Em7   A7   Dm7 G7   C△———

and

II   V

Cm7   F7   B♭m7   E♭7   A♭m7   D♭7   G♭m7   B7   Em7   A7   Dm7 G7   C△———

or

II   V

Bm7   E7   Am7   D7   Gm7   C7   Fm7   B♭7   E♭m7   A♭7   D♭m7   G♭7   B△

16

and

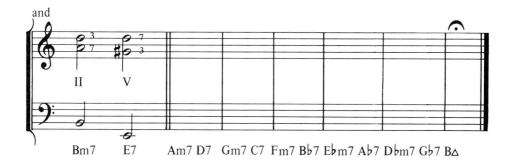

Bm7   E7   Am7 D7 Gm7 C7 Fm7 B♭7 E♭m7 A♭7 D♭m7 G♭7 B△

(iii) Minor 7th to dominant 7th to major 7th (II – V – I):

Ex. 18

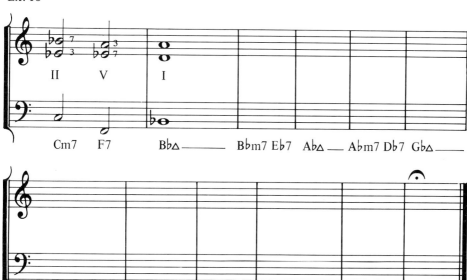

Cm7   F7   B♭△ ——   B♭m7 E♭7 A♭△ ——   A♭m7 D♭7 G♭△ ——

G♭m7   B7   E△ ——   Em7 A7 D△ ——   Dm7 G7 C△

and

Cm7   F7   B♭△—— B♭m7 E♭7 A♭△—— A♭m7 D♭7 G♭△——

17

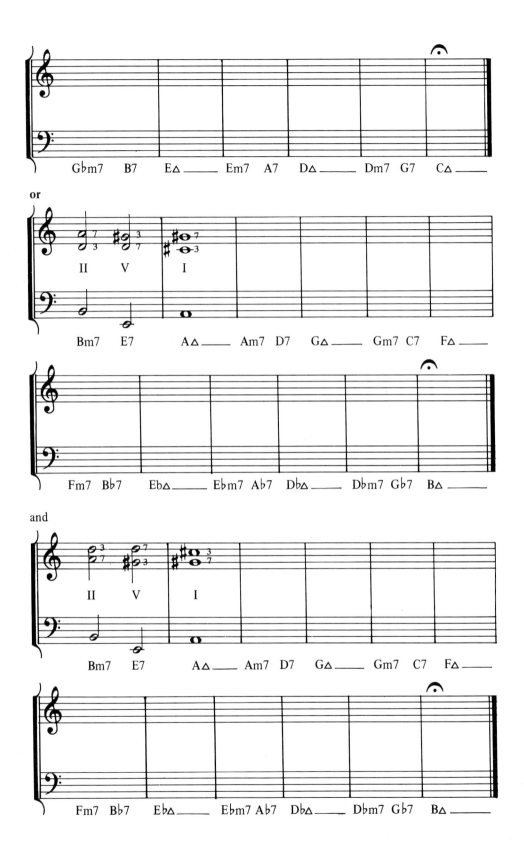

or

and

3 MORE CHORD TYPES

Here are three more chord-types:

(i)   Diminished 7th, symbol 'o':

(ii)   Half-diminished 7th, symbol 'φ'

(iii) Minor/major 7th, symbol 'mΔ'.

Types (i) and (ii) are both diminished triads with a different added 7th. The diminished 7th adds a *diminished 7th* above the root (the usual notation making the top note a major 6th, as shown); the half-diminished 7th adds a *minor 7th* above the root (making it a minor 7th chord with a flat 5th). The half-diminished 7th is sometimes symbolized $Cm7^{(b5)}$.

Type (iii) is a minor triad which adds a *major 7th* above the root.

19

Function of the Diminished Chord

The usual function of the diminished chord is to be a chromatic link between two diatonic chords lying a tone apart, either in an ascending or descending progression. In three-part voicing, leave out the diminished 5th, i.e.:

Ex. 19

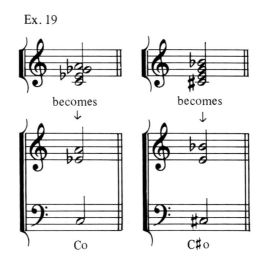

becomes ↓   becomes ↓

Co   C♯o

resulting in:

C△   C♯o   Dm7 D♯o   Em7 E♭o   Dm7 G7

Function of the half-diminished chord

The half-diminished chord does the same job as the minor 7th chord, functioning as a II chord in a II–V–I progression. For this reason the half-diminished is best thought of as a minor 7th chord with flattened 5th. To be recognisable in three-part voicing, the 3rd rather than the 5th must be left out:

20

Ex. 20

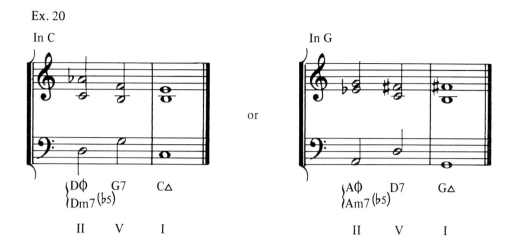

or

An ordinary minor chord without 5th will do the same job as a half-diminished, and so can be used instead.

Function of the minor/major 7th chord

This is parallel to that of the major 7th chord, that is, as a tonic harmony. Sometimes, however, a minor 7th chord can be preferable as a minor tonic harmony. In three-part voicing, leave out the 5th:

Ex. 21

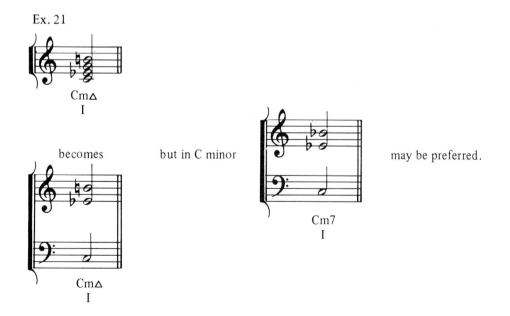

Added 6th Chords

These are major or minor triads, which add a major 6th above the root:

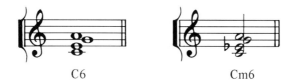

Added 6th chords are mainly used as tonic harmony either instead of, or perhaps more often as a resolution of major 7th chords (major 7th falling to major 6th). In three-part voicing, omit the 5th:

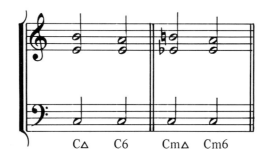

On its own, and especially when voiced in close position, the major added 6th chord has a rather obnoxious blandness and deserves to be castigated as a 'dance band' chord. The minor added 6th chord, though, is more interesting and atmospheric because of the tritone interval between 3rd and 6th. Lester Young was particularly partial to the melodic use of the major 6th against a minor chord.

Extending the Sequence

The first eight bars of *Autumn Leaves* include the three basic kinds of 7th chord, forming a tonal sequence. The complete *Autumn Leaves* sequence is 32 bars long, divided into four eight-bar sections. At its simplest, the whole sequence can use only the three kinds of 7th chord, *i.e.* major, minor and dominant 7ths. However, the chord used in bars 5, 9, 7 and 21 should be half-diminished (as shown in brackets).

Cm7	F7	Bb△	Eb△	Am7 (A∅)	D7	Gm7	Gm7
[Middle Eight] Am7 (A∅)	D7	Gm7	Gm7	Cm7	F7	Bb△	Eb△
[Last Eight] Am7 (A∅)	D7	Gm7	Gm7	Am7 (A∅)	D7	Gm7	Gm7

FINE

Even in three parts, the basic sequence can be given more variety by introducing minor/major 7th, diminished and added-6th chords.

The two bars of Gm7 at the end of the first, second and last eight-bar sections could become:

Ex. 22

(In either case, the two upper parts can be inverted so that the inner movement appears in the highest part.)

23

It is also customary for the two bars of Gm7 in the third and fourth bars of the last eight to be replaced by a descending half-bar progression:

Ex. 23

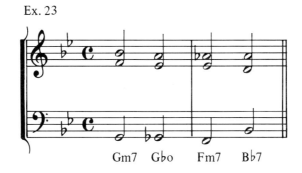

Gm7   G♭o   Fm7   B♭7

Memorising Chord Sequences

Fluent memorisation of chord sequences and their possible variations is essential for coherent improvisation. The basic sequence for *Autumn Leaves* can be memorised in the following stages:

(i) Form: 32 bars in four eight-bar sections ('eights').

　　　1st eight: designate as A
　　　2nd eight: the same A
　　　3rd eight: different, therefore designate as B
　　　4th eight: different again, therefore designate as C

The overall form in eights is therefore:

　　　　　　A   A   B   C

(ii) Subdivide the first eight into two four-bar sections:

　　(a)   IIm7 V7 IΔ IVΔ in B♭;
　　(b)   IIm7 V7 Im7 Im7 in G minor.

Then note that the third (middle) eight simply reverses these two sections; and that the last eight is the second four-bar section twice. The picture to memorise now becomes:

　　　　　　A   (a)   (b)
　　　　　　A   (a)   (b)
　　　　　　B   (b)   (a)
　　　　　　C   (b)   (b)

Having memorised the basic sequence in this way, it should then be possible to insert the possible variations discussed above in the appropriate two-bar 'slots'.

Octave Doublings

The three-part minimal voicings for all the chord types so far discussed (except for the half-diminished chord) can be strengthened on the keyboard by doubling one of the two upper voices in octaves:

Ex. 24

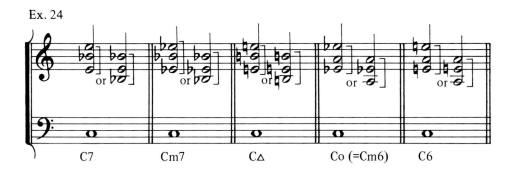

Roots can obviously also be strengthened by octave doubling.

Exercises

On the keyboard:

(i)   Practise all the progressions given in the exercises on pages 15–18 with octave doublings of either upper part.

(ii)   Memorise the basic sequence of *Autumn Leaves* in three-part minimal voicings. Then practise octave doublings of either upper part.

(iii) Incorporate into *Autumn Leaves* the two-bar section variations on pages 23–4, first in three parts, then with octave doublings of either upper part.

4   THE TWELVE-BAR BLUES SEQUENCE

Gaining a deep understanding of the content (feeling) and form of the blues in all its aspects—melodic and rhythmic as well as harmonic—is an essential part of the development of any jazz musician. What follows is only a brief introduction to one aspect of the blues: its harmonic structure. Of course this can scarcely begin to do justice to the blues as a musical form which reaches back to the prehistory of Afro-American music and which remains at the emotional core of jazz. A mere abstract of blues harmony cannot convey the significance of the blues. Those for whom this is a first introduction to the blues must therefore be prepared to go well beyond the information given here.

The simplest twelve-bar blues has the following form:

I7	I7	I7	I7
IV7	IV7	I7	I7
V7	V7	I7	I7

However, today such a blues sequence if played literally would only be suitable for the most obvious kind of rock-and-roll. At least as early as the 1920s the blues as played by e.g. Bessie Smith and Louis Armstrong was becoming harmonically more flexible and subtle through the use of passing chords.

Even without passing chords, the simple form just given would often be varied as follows:

I7	IV7	I7	I7
IV7	IV7	I7	I7
V7	IV7	I7	I7

The use of the subdominant (IV7) in the second bar is standard for most blues performances. In the last four bars, the fall from V7 to IV7 before the final return to I7 is perhaps most typical of a slow blues.

Endings

In the last bar or half-bar V7 is usually played to lead back to the beginning of the sequence. In the blues and in many other jazz sequences this is called a 'turnaround'. The simplest kind of turnaround in the last two bars is

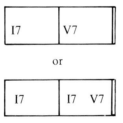

I7	V7

or

I7	I7 V7

Elaborated, this may become either:

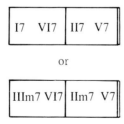

I7 VI7	II7 V7

or

IIIm7 VI7	IIm7 V7

These may be called 'regular turnarounds' and are used not only for a blues but in any sequence beginning with chord I where the last two bars are basically also chord I. Final endings usually arrive at chord I on the last half-bar, though a typical final ending for a blues is this bass figure under chord I in the whole bar:

Ex. 25

F7   Bb7   Bo   F   F7

★Note that both these bass notes are part of the chord of F.

Internal Blues Variations

There are many possible internal variations of the blues sequence, using chords other than I, IV and V. The main purpose of these internal variations is to link the second four to the last four bars in a way which avoids a straight change from I to V between bars eight and nine. The simplest way of achieving this is to use chord VI7 in bar eight to lead (via the cycle of 4ths) to chord II7 or IIm7 in bar nine and to V7 in bar ten (delaying the arrival of V by one bar):

I7	IV7	I7	I7
IV7	IV7	I7	VI7
II7 or IIm7	V7	I7 VI7	IIm7 V7

                              └── Turnaround ──┘

Notice that the four chords in bars 7 to 10 are now the same as the four half-bar chords which make up the turnaround. (In both cases chord II can have a major or minor 3rd).

This variation can be made more supple by using the II – V principle (see page 14)—that is, by using minor 7th chords to precede the important 7th-chord movements in bars 4 to 5 and 8 to 9:

28

I7	IV7	I7	Vm7 I7
IV7	IV7	I7	IIIm7 VI7
II7 or IIm7	V7	I7 VI7	IIm7 V7

The 'II–V' function initiated by these three minor 7th chord additions is clearer if the above numerical chord symbols are translated into letter symbols in a specific key:

Key F F7	B♭7	F7	Key B♭ Cm7 F7 II V
B♭7	B♭7	F7	Key G or Gm Am7 D7 II V
{G7 {Gm7	C7	F7 D7	Gm7 C7

The next important variation is the use of the diminished chord a semitone above IV (♯IV) to link IV to I in bars 2–3 and 6–7:

F7	B♭7 Bo	$\frac{F7}{C}$	Cm7 F7
B♭7	B♭7 Bo	$\frac{F7}{C}$ B♭7	Am7 D7
Gm7	C7	F7 D7	Gm7 C7

29

To avoid an awkward jump in the bass line from B to F, the Bo leads upwards to F7, with C in the bass ($\frac{F7}{C}$). After the same thing happens in bars 7–8, a passing Bb7 can be added in the second half of bar 8 to lead downwards by step to the Am7 in the next bar. This blues sequence would be an appropriate accompaniment to a typical 'modern' or bebop blues, *e.g. Now's the Time*, or *Billie's Bounce* (Charlie Parker).

Here is a tabulation of the variations so far used, in the key of F, to compare with the 'absolutely basic' blues:

(i)   Absolutely basic blues (chords I7, IV7 and V7 only):

F7	F7	F7	F7
Bb7	Bb7	F7	F7
C7	C7	F7	F7

(ii) Rearrangement of absolutely basic blues. IV7 in 2nd bar is standard for most blues; V7 to IV7 in the last four bars is common for slow blues:

F7	Bb7	F7	F7
Bb7	Bb7	F7	F7
C7	Bb7	F7	C7

(iii) Using cycle of 4ths to link the second four to the last four bars, plus a turnaround in the last two bars:

F7	Bb7	F7	F7
Bb7	Bb7	F7	D7
}G7 /Gm7	C7	F7 D7	Gm7 C7

└──Turnaround──┘

30

(iv) Using minor 7th chords to prepare important 7th-chord movements on the II – V principle:

F7	Bb7	F7	Cm7 F7
Bb7	Bb7	F7	Am7 D7
Gm7	C7	{F7 D7 {Am7	Gm7 C7

(v) Using the diminished chord on ♯IV to link subdominant to tonic:

F7	Bb7	F7 — C	Cm7 F7
Bb7	Bb7 Bo	F7 Bb7 — C	Am7 D7
Gm7	C7	{F7 D7 {Am7	Gm7 C7

Exercises

On the keyboard:

(i) At a medium, steady tempo, practise and memorise the five blues sequences given above in three-note minimal voicings:

(a) with $\begin{smallmatrix}3\\7\\1\end{smallmatrix}$ voicing (first chord) leading to $\begin{smallmatrix}7\\3\\1\end{smallmatrix}$ (second chord);

(b) with $\begin{smallmatrix}7\\3\\1\end{smallmatrix}$ voicing (first chord) leading to $\begin{smallmatrix}3\\7\\1\end{smallmatrix}$ (second chord).

Each sequence should be practised separately. Then all five should be played *segue*, in any order.

(ii) Add octave doublings of either upper part (3 or 7), making four-note chords.

5 TRITONE SUBSTITUTION

The interval of a 'tritone' spans three whole tones and divides the octave in half. It is written either as a diminished (flattened) 5th or an augmented 4th:

or   or

'Tritone substitution' is the replacement of any dominant 7th-type chord in a sequence with the same chord type a tritone away. In the key of C, V7 may be substituted by ♭II7:

Tritone

G7   D♭7
V7   ♭II7

Play this substitution at the keyboard and you will find, through your fingers, that the two chords share two common notes, the third and the seventh. Only the bass changes by the interval of a tritone.

Use of tritone substitution

Tritone substitutes are usually used as optional replacements for dominant 7th-type chords which are behaving as dominants in a

33

sequence, *i.e.* resolving to a chord a 4th above. The result is to substitute a bass line descending in semitones for one which moves through the cycle of 4ths, as in:

Em7   A7   Dm7   G7   C△

which becomes, with tritone substitutes:

Em7   Eb7   Dm7   Db7   C△

In this way, any destination which can be reached in a certain number of 4th steps can be reached in the same number of semitone (downward) steps. The significance of tritone substitutes may be appreciated at the end of the second progression above, where Db7 is the tritone substitute for the dominant 7th chord of the key of C, i.e. G7. At the same time, Db7 is the 'true' dominant of Gb, a key very remote from C. The effect of dominant tritone substitution is to imply a momentary modulation to a key far from the one you are actually going to. Its impact is in inverse proportion to its frequency and tritone substitution should *not* be used at every opportunity.

II – V Tritone Substitution

Tritone substitution can be taken a stage further by preceding a dominant tritone substitute chord with the minor 7th chord a 4th below—another tritone substitute—to form a II–V relationship in a remote key from the destination key.

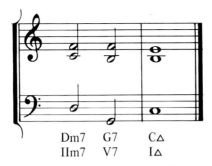

Dm7 G7 CΔ
IIm7 V7 IΔ

becomes, with tritone substitutes:

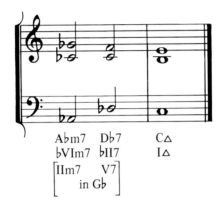

A♭m7 D♭7 CΔ
♭VIm7 ♭II7 IΔ
[IIm7   V7]
    in G♭

This device, said to have been invented by Dizzy Gillespie, reinforces the passing suggestion of being in the most remote key from the actual destination.

Exercises

Play the following examples, to become familiar with the effect of tritone substitutes as shown in the lower chords (three-part voicings):

(i)   Dominant (V) substitution:

Autumn Leaves (first eight)

Cm7	F7	B♭Δ (B♭7)	E♭Δ	Am7	D7	Gm7	Gm7
	B7	(E7)			A♭7		

35

Blues in F

F7 F7
     B7
	B♭7	F7	Cm7 F7
			        B7

B♭7	B♭7 E7	Am7	D7 A♭7

Gm7	C7
	G♭7
		F7 D7
		      A♭7
			Gm7 C7
			        G♭7

(ii)   II – V substitution:

Autumn Leaves (first eight)

Cm7	F7 G♭m7 B7	B♭△ Bm7 E7	E♭△	Am7	D7 E♭m7 A♭7	Gm7	Gm7

Blues in F

F7	B♭7	F7	Cm7 F7 F♯m7 B7
B♭7	B♭7	F7	Am7 D7 E♭m7 A♭7
Gm7	C7 D♭m7 G♭7	F7 D7 A♭7	Gm7 C7 D♭m7 G♭7

6 EXTENSIONS

The three basic types of the 7th chord so far discussed—'straight' (dominant-type) 7th, minor 7th and major 7th—are four-note chords built up in thirds. By continuing upwards in thirds each of these chords can be extended to include seven notes: the four notes of the basic chord (root, 3rd, 5th, 7th) plus the three extensions of the 9th, 11th and 13th.

Ex. 26

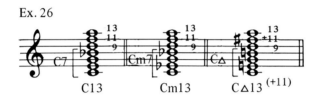

In the dominant 13th (e.g. C13) and minor 13th (Cm13) chords, the three extensions can be thought of as forming a minor triad a 9th (octave and tone) above the root. This superimposed triad is a minor one because its middle note is the 'natural' 11th of the basic chord—an octave and a perfect 4th above the root.

In the major 7th/13th chord (C∆13^{+11}) the superimposed triad formed by the three extensions is a major one because the middle note is the augmented 11th ($^{+11}$) of the basic chord—an octave and an augmented 4th above the root. An augmented 11th can also be included in a dominant 13th chord, which then also appears to be completed by a major triad a 9th above the root:

Ex. 27

Apart from the three basic kinds of 7th chord, half-diminished and minor/major 7th chords can also be extended to 13ths:

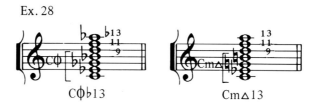

Ex. 28

CØ♭13   Cm△13

In the half-diminished 13th chord the three extensions form a diminished triad a 9th above the root because the 13th is flattened. In the minor/major 13th chord the three extensions form a minor triad a 9th above the root.

Augmented 5th/flat 13th chords

A plus sign (+) following a chord symbol indicates that the 5th is to be augmented (i.e. raised a semitone):

Ex. 29

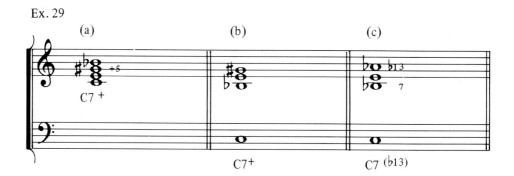

In this example

(a)   shows the dominant 7th augmented chord in block, 'theoretical' voicing,

(b)   shows the same chord as it might normally be voiced, and

(c)   shows the same chord written as a flat 13th chord (i.e. $g^\sharp$ is notated $a^\flat$).

Whichever way it is written it is simplest always to call it a '7th augmented' chord.

7th augmented chords are also possible on minor 7th, major 7th and half-diminished chords:

38

Ex. 30

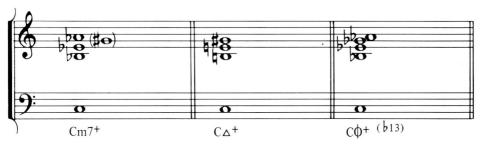

Cm7+   C△+   Cɸ+ (♭13)

The augmented 5th on the minor 7th 'looks' better written as a flat 13th. It *must* be written as a flat 13th on the half-diminished 7th, since this chord already contains a flat 5th—the same note cannot be written as simultaneously flat and sharp. (This is just another case of the orthography of written music getting in the way of what is perfectly clear to the ear on the keyboard.)

Flattened 5th Chords

You have already met the minor 7th/flat 5th chord under the guise of the half-diminished chord (see page 19). Flattened 5ths may also be added to dominant and major 7th chords:

Ex. 31

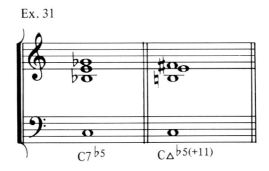

C7♭5   C△♭5(+11)

The flat 5ths on these chords could equally well be seen as augmented 11ths: in the major 7th/flat 5th chord, the flat 5th looks better written as an augmented 11th because the interval between it and the major 7th is then clearly seen as a perfect 5th. Nonetheless, these chords are best described as flattened 5th chords because they include only root, 3rd, flat 5th and 7th, without any extensions.

It is worth noting that the dominant 7th/flat 5th chord includes exactly the same notes as its tritone substitute:

Ex. 32

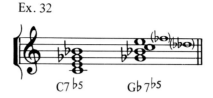

Augmented and Flattened 9th Chords

A '+9' following the symbol for a dominant 7th chord means that the 9th is to be raised a semitone:

Ex. 33

As the example shows, this chord is usually written as a 'flat 10th' chord (i.e. as including both major and minor 3rds in different octaves). This description is best when the chord is used, as it often is, as tonic harmony in a blues. An augmented 9th chord may also include an augmented 5th, written either as a sharp 5th with sharp 9th or as a flat 6th with flat 10th i.e. all added notes sharp or all added notes flat:

Ex. 34

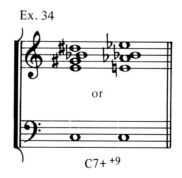

A '♭9' following the symbol for a dominant 7th-type chord means that
the 9th is to be lowered a semitone:

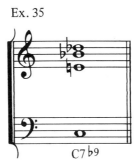

Ex. 35

C7♭9

7   VOICE-LEADING:
FOUR AND FIVE PARTS

Voice-leading in Four Parts

Extensions add colour and texture to individual chords. But, like the lower parts of a chord (3rd and 7th) they also have a leading function which normally requires them to move economically to a nearby note in the next chord. This can best be demonstrated by adding notes one at a time to progressions in basic three-part voicings and hearing how the additions follow through.

5th to 9th Principle

Use again a II – V – I – IV progression in B♮ (the first four chords of the *Autumn Leaves* sequence). Begin by adding the 5th (which is not an extension) above a minimally-voiced chord II, and repeat this note over the following chord:

Ex. 36

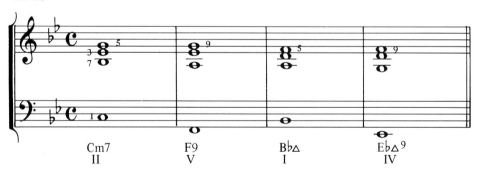

In such a progression, moving by 4ths, the 5th leads to the 9th (applying the 'least movement' principle). Over the first four chords of *Autumn Leaves*, this procedure sets up a pattern of alternating 5ths and 9ths. For the next three chords (II – V – I to G minor) the same alternation applies, but with modified 5ths and 9ths:

Ex. 37

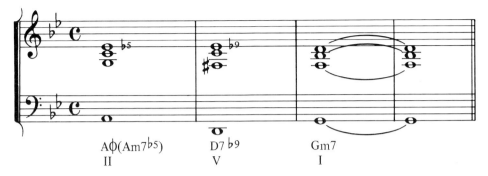

or

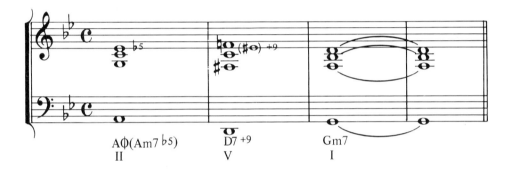

The possible 5th to 9th movements over minor 7th to dominant 7th (II – V) progressions are:

(i)   5th to 9th
(ii)   5th to flat 9th
(iii) 5th to augmented 9th
(iv)   flat 5th to flat 9th
(v)   flat 5th to augmented 9th

Ex. 38

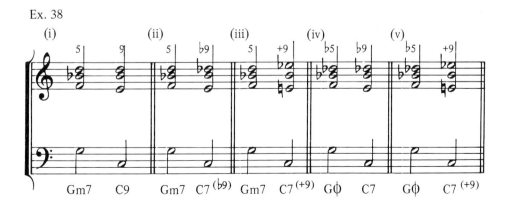

Exercise

Here is a cycle-of-4ths progression of II – V chords voiced in three parts. Add a fourth part above to make the various kinds of 5th to 9th movement as listed in Example 38, leading each possibility through the complete cycle. Repeat these exercises through a cycle up a semitone (beginning on A♭m7).

Ex. 39

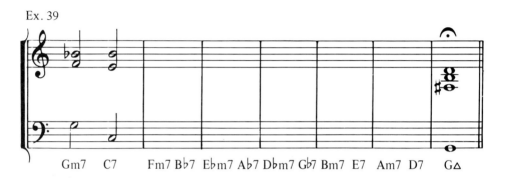

Gm7 C7   Fm7 B♭7 E♭m7 A♭7 D♭m7 G♭7 Bm7 E7   Am7 D7   G△

9th to 13th Principle

The 5th to 9th principle introduced the 5th as the highest part of a chord, above a 1 – 7 – 3 voicing. Over a 1 – 3 – 7 voicing, the 9th can be introduced above the 7th to establish another leading principle:

Ex. 40

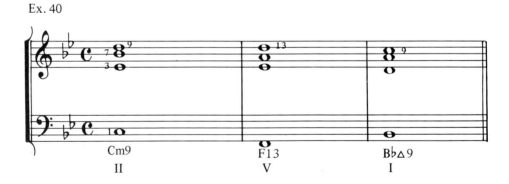

Cm9   F13   B♭△9
II   V   I

Here the 9th leads by 'least movement' (i.e. no movement) to the 13th. In cycle-of-4ths sequences this principle works best on minor 7th to dominant 7th (II – V) movements (as above) or on two dominant-type 7ths:

44

Ex. 41

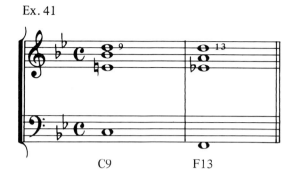

C9   F13

Variations

In working out the variations of 'least movement' voice-leading of 9ths over 4th progressions, start with no movement (as in the two examples above) and then try moving by step (tone or semitone) or even a minor 3rd. In this way, the 9th leads to:

(a)   flat 13th (=augmented 5th)
(b)   perfect 5th
(c)   flat 5th (=augmented 11th)

Ex. 42

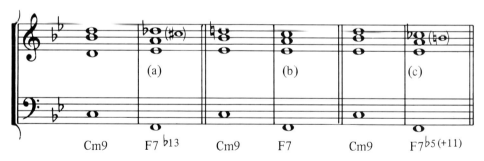

Cm9   F7 ♭13   Cm9   F7   Cm9   F7♭5(+11)

Of the above possibilities, 9th to perfect 5th is the least interesting because the 5th on F7 makes the chord too consonant; it includes only one discord, the 7th, in contrast to the preceding chord which has two (7th and 9th). But if these two chords are turned into *major* 7ths, the leading of the 7th to 5th is well worth exploring.

If you apply 'no movement' and then 'movement by step' to the augmented 9th, you will play:

Ex. 43

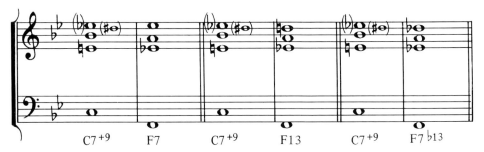

The leading possibilities of the 9th in a four-part cycle of 4ths are:

(i)   9th to 13th (e.g. Cm9 F13)

(ii) 9th to augmented 5th/flat 13th (e.g. Cm9 F7+)

(iii) 9th to 5th (e.g. Cm9 F7, or B♭Δ9 E♭Δ)

(iv) 9th to flat 5th (e.g. Cm9 F7♭5)

(v)   Augmented 9th to 7th (e.g. C7+9 F7)

(vi) Augmented 9th to 13th (e.g. C7+9 F13)

(vii) Augmented 9th to flat 13th/augmented 5th (e.g. C7+9 F7+)

(viii) Flat 9th to augmented 5th (e.g. A7♭9 D7+)

Exercise

Play cycles-of-4th progressions in each of these voice-leads.

Voice-leading in Five Parts

The same principles can be initiated in five-part chords by adding both 5th and 9th in the starting chord either to a $1-7-3$ minimal voicing:

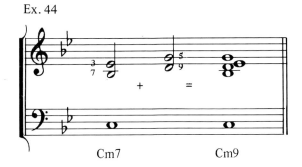

Ex. 44

Cm7   Cm9

or to a 1 – 3 – 7 minimal voicing:

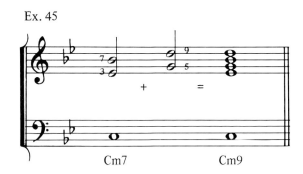

Ex. 45

Cm7   Cm9

Either of these starting chords sets up the 'double leading principle' of 5th to 9th and 9th to 13th, like this:

Ex. 46

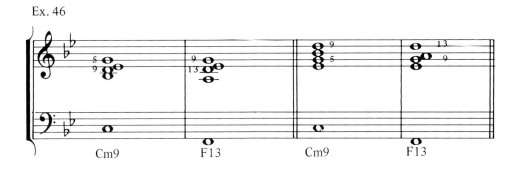

Cm9   F13   Cm9   F13

This double leading principle can be 'driven' through a cycle-of-4ths progression such as the first eight bars of *Autumn Leaves*. The possible variations of 5th to 9th and 9th to 13th movements listed on pages 43 and 46 provide a number of alternative voicings for the dominant 7th chords in this progression:

(i)   added to 1–3–7 dominant 7ths:

Ex. 47a

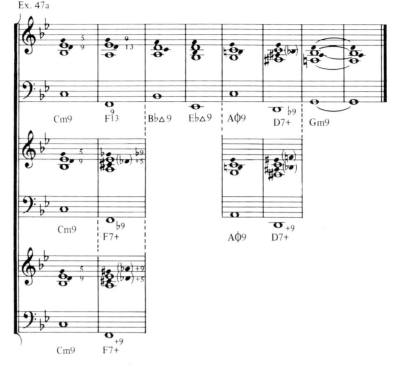

(ii)   added to 1–7–3 dominant 7ths:

Ex. 47b

Voice-leading Minor 11ths

The natural 11th is most at home as an extension of a minor 7th chord. In four parts, the 11th can appear above either a $1-7-3$ or a $1-3-7$ minimal voicing:

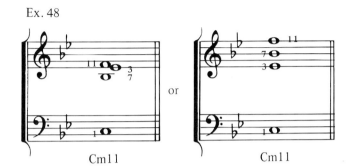

In either case, the 'least-movement' leading of the 11th in a $II-V$ progression is to the root of the V chord:

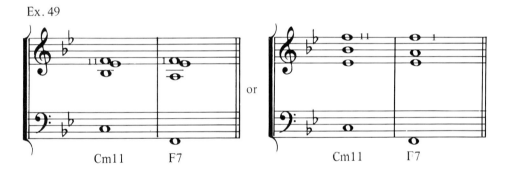

In these examples, the gritty texture of the minor 11th chord is lost when it is resolved onto the slightly weak doubled-root V chord. One way to avoid this loss of tension is to resolve instead to the tritone substitute, so that the 11th leads to the flat 5th:

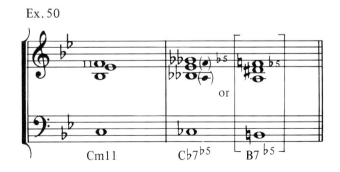

49

In five parts, the texture of the minor 11th chord is made denser either by doubling the 3rd or by including the 9th over a 1−3−7 voicing. The higher 3rd or the 9th then leads to the 13th (which as a strong dissonance compensates for the doubled root of the V chord):

Ex. 51

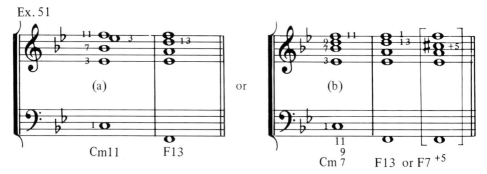

Over a II−V movement the 11th might also lead upwards to a flat 9th or an augmented 9th. The second of these possibilities is perhaps the most effective in a II−V−I context:

Ex. 52

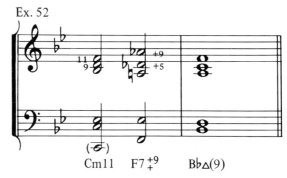

An 11th over a half-diminished (i.e. minor 7th/flat 5th) chord can be voiced, in five parts, to include the 9th but leaving out the 3rd. This is a rare exception to the general rule that 3rds should be included. In this example, the flat 5th of the half-diminished chord leads upwards by a tone to the augmented 9th of the following chord:

Ex. 53

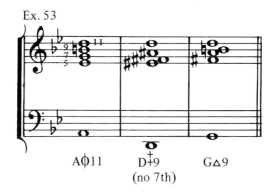

50

8 MORE EXTENSIONS

Dominant Natural 11ths

Although the augmented 11th is preferable in dominant 13th-type chords (see page 37), in dominant 11th chords the natural 11th has a special attraction, voiced as a four-part chord over $1-3-7$:

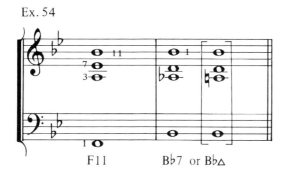

Ex. 54

F11   Bb7 or Bb△

This chord is often to be heard in the music of Thelonious Monk and Stan Tracey.

Augmented 11th/Dominant 13ths

Over a dominant 7th chord, the augmented 11th usually appears together with the 9th and 13th. It can, however, be a four-part chord with the 9th only above a dominant 7th. Voiced in four or five parts the 3rd of $1-3-7$ has to be omitted if the 9th is to be included. In a six-part voicing, the 3rd can be included.

Ex. 55

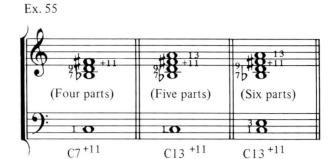

Although richly dissonant, the augmented 11th chord is relatively static. It does not push for resolution in the same way as the augmented 9th chord. For this reason, the augmented 11th tends to be avoided as an extension of a 7th chord which is actually functioning as dominant harmony (i.e. as a V chord in a given key). The most common use of the augmented 11th seems to be as I or IV harmony in a blues and in sequences with blues-like movements, or as chord II harmony. In the latter context, it resolves neatly to an augmented 9th chord:

Ex. 56

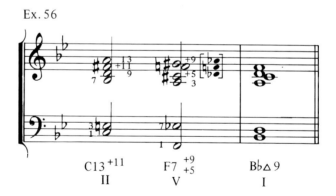

Notice that the major triad on top of chord II simply moves down a semitone. Over a cycle-of-4ths progression in the bass, the upper parts of an augmented 11th chord become the upper parts of an augmented 9th chord simply by moving down a semitone.

Ex. 57

$C13^{+11}$ $F7^{+9}_{+5}$ $Bb13^{+11}$ $Eb7^{+9}_{+5}$ $Ab13^{+11}$

The 'Altered Dominant' 7th

If, in the progression Dm7 G7 CΔ9 (II – V – I in C), you use the tritone substitute Db7 for the G7, the Db7 can be extended to form a 13th chord with 9th and augmented 11th:

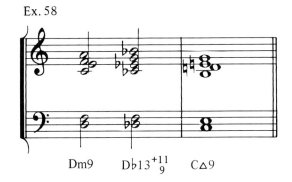

Ex. 58

Dm9 $Db13^{+11}_{9}$ CΔ9

Notice that the augmented 11th of this extended tritone substitute is G, which is also the root of the original V chord. If now you retain all the notes of the extended Db7 chord except for the root Db, and replace the root with the original root, G, the result is a G chord which looks like this:

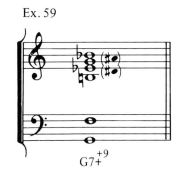

Ex. 59

$G7+^{+9}$

This chord, often called the 'altered dominant', is usually used as a V chord as part of a II – V – I progression (see example 56). In this context IIm7 can be effectively replaced by IIø like this:

Ex. 60

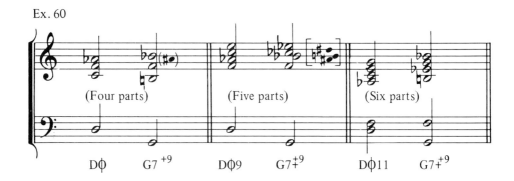

Notice that in six parts, the four upper parts of DøII are transposed up a minor 3rd to become the upper parts of the altered dominant 7th, departing from the 'least movement' principle of voice-leading.

Other Dominant Modifications

Two further modifications of dominant harmony are obtained by combining the flattened 9th either with the 13th, or with 13th and augmented 11th. Here are examples of both possibilities in the context of a II – V – I progression in B♭, first in five then in six parts:

Ex. 61

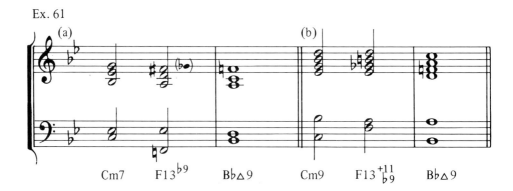

Notice that in (a) the 13th is prepared by the doubled 3rd in the Cm7. The 13th/flat 9th chord is a particularly biting discord because of the combination of this clash with the clash between root and flat 9th. (Both are essentially semitone clashes.) In (b) the 13th is above the flat 9th, and is joined by the augmented 11th approached from the doubled 7th of the Cm7 (moving in contrary motion from the downwards resolution of the lower 7th to the 3rd).

These dominant 13th/flat 9th/augmented 11th chords are such strong discords that they should be used with discretion.

The Suspended 4th

If in the II – V – I progression Dm7 G9 CΔ the bass moves from D to G while the upper parts of the Dm7 are prolonged the resulting harmony is called a suspended 4th chord ('sus 4'). The 7th of Dm7, which would normally resolve down a semitone to the 3rd of G7, becomes the suspended 4th over G9:

Ex. 62

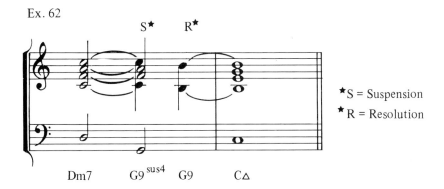

★S = Suspension
★R = Resolution

The chord symbol for G9^sus 4 may be shown more simply as the major triad of the 7th (F) over the dominant root (C), like this:

Ex. 63

In the II – V – I context, the suspended 4th chord usually resolves—as here—by the suspended notes falling to the 3rd. The suspension need not, however, be resolved at all. This leaves the 'suspended 4th' as a chord in its own right. Herbie Hancock used it repeatedly like this:

Ex. 64

9   VOICE-LEADING: SIX PARTS

Each new note that is added to a chord increases the number of ways in which that chord can be voiced and resolved. In six parts there are so many possibilities that it would be impractical to try to list them all. What follows is just an indication of some of the possibilities of six-part voice-leading. Assuming root, 3rd and 7th (or 7th and 3rd) as the underlying voicing, the addition of three more parts will normally include the 9th, 11th and 13th. Such a voicing for a minor 7th chord could be led through the first eight bars of *Autumn Leaves* as follows:

Ex. 65

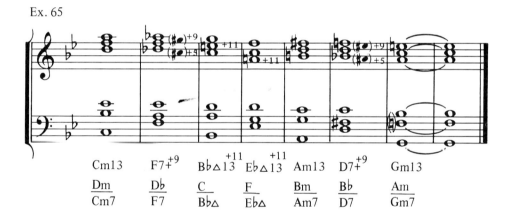

The chord symbols for these six-part voicings can be written out as basic symbol plus numerical extensions (e.g. Cm13, which assumes inclusion of 7th, 9th and 11th) or, more conveniently but less analytically, as triads over basic 7th symbols, e.g. $\dfrac{\text{Dm}}{\text{Cm7}}$ for Cm13 above.

Notice that the three upper parts form superimposed triads including either all three extensions or +9, root and +5. These triads usually lead by least movement to the nearest available superimposed triad on the next chord. (A break in this principle is allowed between bars 4 and 5 as bar 5 begins a new harmonic phrase, II – V – I to G minor.) It is difficult to reconcile the principle of 'least-movement' voice-leading with avoiding the octave doubling of one part in six parts. In the resolution of $\dfrac{\text{Dm}}{\text{Cm7}}$ to $\dfrac{\text{D}\flat}{\text{F7}}$ the 11th of the first chord unavoidably becomes the doubled root of the second.

Superimposed triads formed in six-part voicings can themselves appear in any triadic inversion, leading to the nearest inversion of the next superimposed triad:

Ex. 66

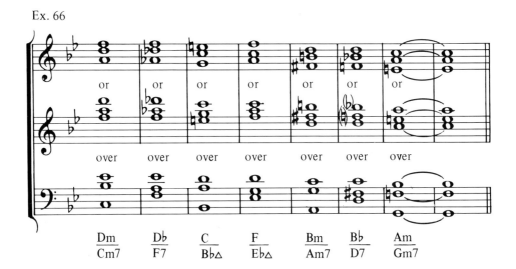

Exercise

Practise cycle-of-4th progressions of superimposed triads on 7th chords in six parts, using different inversions of the upper triad in the right hand as in the last example.

PART TWO

10   BLUES TONALITY: C

The twelve-bar blues in its simplest three-chord form (see page 26), is probably the most natural starting point for beginners in jazz improvisation. While blues phrasing using the notes of the blues scale is only a part of the total repertoire of jazz phraseology it is fundamental, and a sense of blues tonality pervades the whole of jazz. Unless the music is to lose its emotional identity the ability to play a convincing blues will remain an inescapable test of authenticity for any aspiring jazz musician.

It is perhaps best to regard the blues scale as consisting of two distinct pentatonic (five-note) scales, the major and the minor, plus the flattened 5th (or raised 4th) as an important additional note:

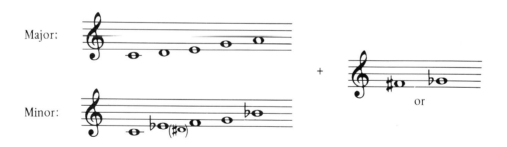

These two pentatonic forms, together with the flat 5th, can be combined to make a composite, nine-note blues scale:

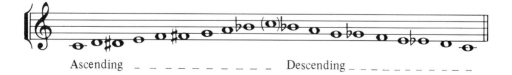

The relationship between these notes and the three chords (chapter 4) of the basic twelve-bar blues sets up the characteristic effects of blues tonality.

The most important notes of the blues scale are the so-called 'blue' notes: the flat 3rd, flat 7th and flat 5th. Sounded against the three blue chords, each of these notes has its own emotional and harmonic significance.

Flat 3rd

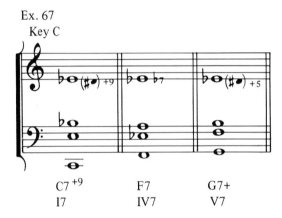

Ex. 67
Key C

C7^{+9} F7   G7+
I7   IV7   V7

Over the tonic chord, the blue 3rd clashes with the major 3rd of the chord, setting up, harmonically speaking, an augmented 9th (or flat 10th) chord. The 'minor–major' effect of this clash is the most distinctive feature of blues tonality.

Over IV7, the blue 3rd doubles the 7th of the chord. This relationship is less dissonant than the major 7th clash of the same note with the major 3rd of I7: if the blue 3rd is sustained over the movement of I7 to IV7, the effect is of resolution.

Over V7, the blue 3rd sounds as an augmented 5th. This is more dissonant than the same note on IV7, since it forms a flat 7th with the 7th of the chord (discord on discord), but it is less dissonant than the blue 3rd on I7: if the blue 3rd is sustained over V7 to I7, the effect is a kind of 'reverse' resolution which intensifies the dissonance.

Flat 7th

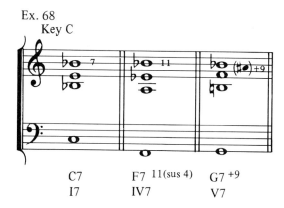

Ex. 68
Key C

C7   F7 11(sus 4)   G7 +9
I7   IV7   V7

The blue 7th on I7 doubles the 7th of the chord, duplicating on the tonic the effect of the blue 3rd on IV7.

The blue 7th on IV7 creates a new relationship, the 11th or 4th. Sustained or repeated over I7 to IV7, the effect of the blue 7th is one of suspension (see example 62).

The blue 7th on V7 duplicates on the dominant the effect of the blue 3rd on I7, creating a dominant augmented 9th chord. Sustained or repeated over V7 to I7, this blue 7th's effect is of resolution, parallel to the effect of the blue 3rd over I7 to IV7.

Flat 5th

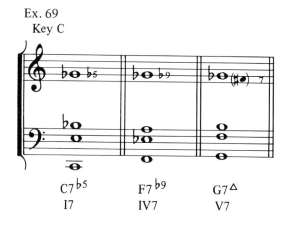

Ex. 69
Key C

C7 b5   F7 b9   G7 △
I7   IV7   V7

The blue 5th forms a stable interval only on I7. On IV7 it forms a flat 9th which 'asks' to resolve upwards or downwards a semitone, to the root or major 9th of the chord. On V7, the blue 5th is, on the face of it, an extremely wrong note, as it forms a major 7th(Δ) which clashes with the flat 7th of the chord. However, this note is quite viable in the context of a blues phrase over V7 to I7 (the concluding cadence of a blues).

From this, it is clear that the three blue notes (flat 3rd, 7th and 5th) are capable of forming a number of subtle melodic and harmonic relationships with the three basic blues chords.

A A1 B: a basic blues improvisation

A simple (though not quite the simplest) twelve-bar blues has the following sequence in C (see chapter 4):

C7	F7	C7	C7
C7	F7	C7	C7
F7	F7	C7	C7
G7	G7 (F7)	C7	C7 G7

Here is one chorus of a possible improvisation on this basic blues sequence, in 'classic' blues style. Play the harmonic sequence first, then sing or play the melody over it.

Ex. 70

C7   F7   C7   C7

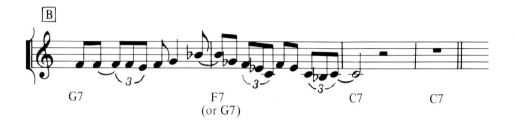

This example follows the traditional format of a vocal blues. It is cast in three four-bar sections, each consisting of a two-and-a-half-bar phrase followed by a space which would have been occupied by an instrumental response.

The first bar of the initial phrase is a motif descending from the blue 7th and arriving at the major 3rd at the half-bar, firmly announcing the tonic chord (C7). Bar two is a slightly lengthened and rhythmically varied version of the same motif, but with the significant difference that it has the blue 3rd at the half-bar, doubling the flat 7th of the harmony (F7). The pivotal notes in these two bars are therefore the blue 7th and blue 3rd. In bar two the blue 7th is momentarily suspended over the harmony. These two motifs form the initial statement of this blues improvisation.

The second four bars begin with the counter-statement, which echoes the statement but is tailored to suit the two bars of IV7 (F7) before returning to the tonic (C7). The blue 3rd on the half-bar is used in both bars instead of bar two only (as it was in the statement). This adjustment, though apparently slight, provides a significant contrast to the initial statement. Otherwise, the variation is only rhythmic.

The last four bars—the resolution—partly contrast and partly recapitulate the statement and counter-statement. The triplet pick-up before bar nine introduces a new motif tailored to the harmony (G7), followed in bar ten by a motif echoing bars two and six, but introducing for the first time the blue 5th, with a low blue 7th before the end.

Exercises

(i)   This simple blues chorus includes all the significant 'blue note' relationships. Use it as a model for similar blues improvisations based on the same three-phrase (statement/counter-statement/ resolution) format, as follows:

Statement: an initial phrase taking up about two and a half bars of the first four bars of a blues, basically tonic but often implying sub-dominant in bar two. Designate this phrase as $\boxed{A}$.

Counter-statement: an answering phrase of similar length for the second four bars, based on the subdominant and returning to the tonic. The counter-statement may be only a slight variation of the statement. Designate as $\boxed{A1}$.

Resolution: a final phrase of similar length for the last four bars, leading from dominant (two bars) to tonic, or from dominant (one bar) via sub-dominant (one bar) to tonic. The resolution is usually a melodic contrast to phrases one and two but may (as in the example above) recapitulate their endings. Designate as $\boxed{B}$.

The form of a twelve-bar blues improvisation constructed in this way is then:

$$\boxed{A} \quad \boxed{A1} \quad \boxed{B}$$

(ii)   This description of the old vocal blues form may seem academic, but the naturalness of the three-phrase form becomes obvious in such a three-line verse form as:

> The blues jumped a rabbit, ran him a solid mile
> Oh the blues jumped a rabbit, ran him a solid mile
> When the blues overtook him, he cried just like a natural child.

Make up a twelve-bar melody to these lyrics, in $A - A1 - B$ form. The melody should be based entirely on the blues scale, and should emphasise the blue-note relationships discussed in this chapter.

Rhythm and 'Feel'

While any literate musician should have no difficulty in *reading* the blues solo on pages 62–3 the rhythmic interpretation, even if metronomically accurate, might well be jerky and unrelaxed. In a word, it might lack a jazz 'feel'. This may partly be due to not understanding that written quavers (at least in slow to moderate tempi) should be interpreted as crotchet-quaver triplets: ♫ = ♩ ♪. This means, in turn, that syncopations written by tying the second half of a beat to the next beat should be played as the last third of a triplet: ♪♩ = ♪♩.

These 'swung' quavers are often incorrectly described as 'dotted' rhythms, as if ♩ ♪ were to be played as ♩. ♫. It is often this particular misconception which is responsible for the jerkiness of attempts at swung quavers.

Such difficulties with jazz rhythm (which are easily avoided by people who know nothing about music) are really symptoms of allowing the habit of reading rhythm to interfere with a natural, that is, bodily articulation of rhythm and pulse. To position jazz rhythms in a way which is both accurate and relaxed, each beat of the pulse must be physically felt, and capable of accurate subdivision. Foot-tapping, though often discouraged in classical training, is a help in jazz.

The basic skill is to be able to combine rhythm and pulse. The combination of any one rhythm and the pulse is actually a simple polyrhythm and, as such, needs to be co-ordinated. For example a quite simple syncopated figure such as ♪ ♩. ♪ ○ can be a problem. This is easily solved by combining the figure with a crotchet pulse to form a resultant:

Figure + Pulse
=
Resultant

Once learned, the resultant can be separated again into figure and pulse as follows:

H: Hand
F: Foot

65

A useful way to practise the rhythms of the blues melody on pages 62–3 is to play through it while someone claps steady triplets. Each note must fall on the correct part of a triplet.

Synchronising Harmony and Rhythm

To interpret a written jazz solo with a good rhythmic feel (though worth practising) is one thing: it is quite another to *improvise* phrases which are at the same time harmonically and rhythmically coherent. For beginners it is often difficult to keep track of both aspects at the same time. The tendency, if you are concentrating on rhythm, is to lose your place in the chord sequence or, if you are concentrating on harmony (i.e. what notes to play on a chord) to lose the beat.

It can be helpful to separate consciously, and then re-combine, the harmonic (note-choosing) and rhythmic (note-positioning) aspects of phrase-making. If you reduce the rhythmic side to an on-the-beat squareness you can concentrate solely on the relationship of the notes to the chords. Treated in this way, the first phrase of the sample blues solo might look like this:

Ex. 71

Take this process a stage further and play the phrase without any pulse at all, concentrating only on the interval formed by each note with its chord—and being aware of this *exactly as each note is played.*

Then practise a similarly focussed awareness of the original rhythm of the phrase by simply clapping the rhythm over a four-square foot-pulse:

Just as you concentrated on the harmony of each note when the phrase was stripped of rhythm, now concentrate on the precise rhythmic position of each note: on what beat, or what parts of each beat, does each note fall?

Once you have concentrated separately on the melodic/harmonic and the rhythmic aspects of the phrase, re-combine the two and you should find it easier to be equally aware of both harmony and rhythm. The hardest part of improvising jazz is to be able to place the notes of a phrase so that they 'work' harmonically and rhythmically. To achieve this you have to be prepared to worry over each phrase like a dog over a bone.

Building a Vocabulary of Phrases

Jazz improvisation, far from being a leap into the dark, is a matter of developing a conscious vocabulary of musical ideas. These ideas or (to use the time-honoured word) 'licks', can be borrowed to begin with from the solos of your favourite musicians by a process of aural analysis, *i.e.* by careful (not casual) listening.

The process of appropriating licks and building them into a coherent improvisation has two essential ingredients:

(i)   An awareness of the context of each newly-acquired phrase: where can you use it in a chord sequence? This involves understanding the relationship of the notes in a phrase to their underlying chord or chords.
(ii) the ability to use the phrase flexibly. Will you stretch or compress the rhythm, change, add or subtract notes to achieve good phrase-to-phrase continuity? Remember that any phrase can be varied rhythmically, melodically, or both.

Of course improvisation is not merely a question of repeating other people's ideas in appropriate contexts. Any lick, once in your repertory, naturally becomes a starting-point for your own individual variations. In this way, what starts as a borrowed idea can be transformed into an original statement.

Rhythmic Variation

Syncopation and avoidance of rhythmic symmetry are characteristic of jazz. But, as suggested on page 66, there is a square version of every rhythmically interesting phrase. A useful way of practising rhythmic variation is to start with a square phrase and apply different rhythmic devices to it. A 'square' melody over the opening of the *Autumn Leaves* sequence might be:

This could be varied *rhythmically* like this:

or like this:

Variation (a) delays the first note and 'pulls back' the third and fourth notes, leaving only the second note 'on the beat':

Variation (b) pulls back the first and fourth notes, leaving the second and third notes on the beat:

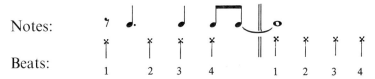

Both these variations illustrate how jazz players use syncopation to avoid duplicating the pulse.

Another common rhythmic variation to experiment is to introduce triplets into melodies which begin as groups of equal ♪ s:

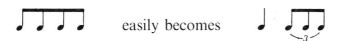 easily becomes

and, if you also delay or pull back one of the four notes:

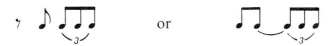 or

Melodic Variations

Continuing the quest for flexibility in improvising you may change, add or subtract notes:

with changed notes may become

with added notes may become

with notes subtracted may become

Ex. 73c

69

Metric Displacement

Moving a phrase backwards or forwards across the bar is a common device (at which Charlie Parker was especially skilled). It counts both as rhythmic and melodic variation since the shift in position alters the rhythmic and harmonic emphasis of the phrase:

Ex. 74

becomes:

Ex. 74a

or:

Ex. 74b

Developing a Blues Solo

Keeping to the basic A A1 B blues form, you may now begin to apply these variation principles, phrase by phrase. Two further variation principles for whole phrases are (a) adaptation and (b) transposition. Both may involve rhythmic and melodic variation but both have harmonic origins.

(a) The blues statement:

Ex. 75

is itself an example of adaptation, where the second bar is basically a repeat of the first but adapted by having a blue 3rd *to suit the harmony* of F7. In the adaptation principle of variation, the register of the phrase remains the same: notes are changed to fit new chords.

(b) Variation by transposition, on the other hand, is the perhaps more obvious tactic of transposing a phrase from one chord to another, changing register as well as notes to suit the new chord and keeping the melodic intervals the same:

Ex. 76

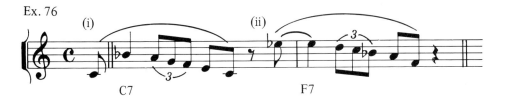

Dealing with chord changes by adapting *or* transposing phrases is a common procedure in jazz improvisation. But there are some pit-falls for the unwary. In the blues, for example, it is perhaps unwise to transpose a phrase featuring the blue 3rd over chord I to the blue 3rd over chord IV:

Ex. 77

The Evolution of the Blues

The three-phrase A A1 B form of melody is only a starting point for blues improvisation. Its importance is that it clearly states the basic form and expressive devices of the blues and so provides a set of guide-lines for more elaborate improvisations within the twelve-bar form. The A A1 B blues form represents the traditional vocal blues, leaving a space of about one and a half bars for an instrumental response at the end of each four-bar section. These responses in a traditional blues tend to be more freely improvised than the initial phrases which they answer.

Harmonically, the blues sequence has been varied by including chords other than I7, IV7 and V7 from at least the 1920s onwards. But even without additional harmonies the combination of the blues scale and the three basic blues chords should be thoroughly investigated. Strictly speaking, pure blues improvisation is not based on chords, but on the blues scale itself, which is coloured by the supporting harmony. It is therefore possible to play the blues without too much consideration of the chord sequence.

This folk-blues approach can also work over additional chords, however, since these can also harmonise with the blues scale. The inclusion of new chords in the twelve-bar sequence adds another layer of melodic possibilities, allowing passages of modulation to link the three sections of the blues. With the advent of modern jazz in the 1940s, the blues regularly included additional chords and became a sort of laboratory for reconciling the raw expression of blues tonality with the sophistication of diatonic-chromatic harmony.

The evolution of the jazz blues is, in microcosm, the development of jazz as a whole: an art-form balancing the folk elements of Afro-American music with the symmetries of Western harmony.

11 BLUES TONALITY: F

Many of the most memorable blues performances in modern jazz have been in the key of F. Here are the basic harmonic changes for a typical modern or bop blues in F, to be a ground for improvisations such as Charlie Parker's *Now's the time* or *Billie's Bounce*. Memorise it.

A	F7	Bb7 Bo	$\frac{F7}{C}$	Cm7 F7
A1	Bb7	Bb7 Bo	$\frac{F7 \quad (Bb7)}{C}$	Am7 D7
B	Gm7	C7	F7 D7	Gm7 C7

└─Turnaround─┘

As a first step, improvise a melody using the basic blues scale (see page 59) over those chords noting how the distinctive notes (flat 3rd, flat 7th, flat 5th) harmonise with them. Listening carefully, hear how the flat 3rd (Ab) sounds as a diminished 7th over Bo (bars two and six), but as an augmented 5th over C7 (bar ten) and as a flat 5th over D7 (bars eight and eleven). The 'additional' chords of modern jazz give the blue 3rd a heightened effect when it does not form part of the chord.

Compare the sound of the tonic (F) which 'fits' every chord; and the 5th (C) which fits every chord but Bo (bars two and six). In improvising melodies like this, the scale-notes are all-important and the chord changes (harmony) are only a source of 'colour'.

II – V – I Change Running

The 'opposite' approach to improvising a modern jazz blues is to allow the chords themselves, either individually or in pairs or groups, to become the generators of melodic ideas. There are two ways of turning chords into melodies: you can construct phrases from the arpeggios of chords; or you can convert chords into scales and construct phrases from the scales. Both approaches are 'vertical' ways of looking at chords. They need to be balanced by an awareness of the 'horizontal' implication of chord movements—in other words, the voice-leading tendency of each note in, and over, a chord.

Taking this into account, here is a typical 'change-running' phrase linking the three chords of a II – V – I movement:

Ex. 78

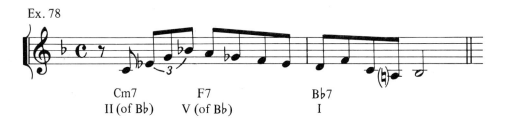

Clearly this phrase is partly arpeggio and partly scale, and also includes the voice-leading of 7th to 3rd ($b^{\flat'}$ to a' from Cm7 to F7 and $e^{\flat'}$ to d' from F7 to B♭7). Such a melodic phrase is produced by reflecting on chords. Now play a whole melody over the *Billie's Bounce* blues changes:

Ex. 79

Here the II – V – I changes are run at three points in the sequence: bars four to five; eight to nine; and twelve to bar one of the next chorus. The melodic notes over each II – V change are clearly suggested by the arpeggios of the chords beneath them. This way of moving towards a 'I' destination over a preceding II – V movement is a leading principle of jazz melodic improvisation.

Phrasing on and towards strong bars

A phrase such as:

Ex. 80

on the first bar of an F blues is an example of sitting a phrase directly on a strong (odd-numbered) bar. Contrast this with a phrase leading from a weak (even-numbered) to a strong bar:

Ex. 81

The two ways of phrasing (on or towards strong bars) can be distinct or they can be combined into a single phrase which approaches a strong bar and then elaborates on it:

Ex. 82

Harmonically, the lead-in to such a phrase can anticipate the chord of a strong bar, even if the chord (or chords) in the preceding bar are different (as in the above examples). On the other hand, the lead-in to a strong bar can be patterned on the chord(s) of the bar before, as in II – V – I change-running.

Interchanging

The three ideas used in playing over II – V – I progressions in an F blues (example 79) were:

Ex. 83
(a)
(b)
(c)

If suitably interchanged and transposed, any one of these ideas would work (in this particular solo) in place of either of the others. For example, phrase (b) or (c), transposed to Cm7—F7 could interchange with (a) in bars four to five, as:

Ex. 84
(b)
(c)

Exercises

(i)   Memorise the F blues solo (example 79) and its chord-changes. Then play the solo but

    (i)   use bar four, transposed, in place of bar eight and bar twelve
    (ii)   use bar eight, transposed, in place of bar four and bar twelve
    (iii) use bar twelve, transposed, in place of bar four and bar eight

(ii)   As for exercise (i), but interchange bars four, eight and twelve suitably transposed, as follows:

    (i)   4 – 12 – 8
    (ii)   8 – 4 – 12
    (iii) 8 – 12 – 4
    (iv) 12 – 4 – 8
    (v)   12 – 8 – 4

(iii) Compose and memorise your own melodic variations on the chord-changes in bars four, eight and twelve. Transpose each variation so that it can be used in place of either of the others. Then repeat exercises (i) and (ii) using these new variations.

(iv) Compose and memorise your own complete F blues solo to include your variations on bars four, eight and twelve, with new improvisation in all the other bars.

(v)   Repeat exercises (i) and (ii) with your new solo, but including the original phrases (a) (b) and (c) instead of your new phrases at these points.

12 THE 'ROUND THE CLOCK' BLUES

The insertion of half-bar II – V movements into the twelve-bar blues is taken to its limit in the so-called 'round the clock' blues, such as Parker's *Blues for Alice* (1951) in F; and *Laird Baird* (1952) in B♭. These changes can be used either for an entire performance or as an optional variation (cued by the soloist) in an ordinary blues.

Round the Clock Blues

Bars 1 - 4:	F△	Em7 A7 (E∅)	Dm7 G7	Cm7 F7
Bars 5 - 8:	B♭△	B♭m7 E♭7	Am7 D7	A♭m7 D♭7
Bars 9 - 12:	Gm7	C7	F△ D7 (Am7)	Gm7 C7

While the main 'stations' of the blues are retained (I, bars one and eleven; IV, bar five; II, bar nine, preparing V) the rest of the sequence consists almost entirely of half-bar II – V movements. Two different kinds of II – V movement are involved. The bass progression of bars two to four follows the cycle of 4ths exactly, to arrive at IV (B♭△) on bar five:

Ex. 85

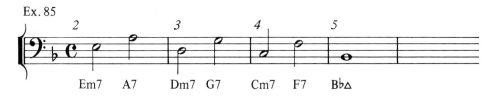

The II – V movements in pairs are each a tone lower than the previous bar (II – Vs in tones).

The II – V movements in bars six to ten are each a semitone lower than the previous bar ('chromatic' II – Vs):

Ex. 86

The two-bar turnaround at the end of the chorus may begin on FΔ or Am7. If it begins on Am7, then the turnaround consists of half-bar II – Vs in tones.

Altogether, the round-the-clock blues is a study in improvising over II – Vs in tones and chromatic II – Vs—while at the same time preserving the emotional force of the blues. In *Blues for Alice* and *Laird Baird*, Charlie Parker achieves this by a combination of running the changes and finding appropriate spaces in the sequence in which to fit 'pure' blues phrases.

The following solo on the clock changes in F is a study in running the changes rather than in alternating or combining this approach with blues phrasing. The solo is an almost continuous phrase, but it can also be viewed as including a number of one-bar 'licks' each fitting a II – V movement. These are labelled (a) to (f). The requirements for producing such a solo therefore include:

(i)   having a sufficient stock of II – V ideas on call to cover the sequence and

(ii) being able to link these to achieve melodic continuity from bar to bar.

Ex. 87

A detailed analysis will reveal that:

(i)   Bars one to three contain three separate ideas—a tonic centre phrase on FΔ, followed by two different II – V phrases (a) and (b) on Em7–A7 and Dm7–G7. All three ideas are drawn from a stock of practised phrases, but the choice of particular phrases for each bar is dictated by the need for melodic balance and continuity. What has just happened influences what is to happen next. The wide downwards interval of the solo's first two notes is balanced by two smaller upwards intervals, and the arpeggiated form of the first half-bar is balanced by the downwards scale movement of the second half-bar. This downwards movement subconsciously decides the particular choice of a II – V phrase starting on the 5th of the first chord in bar two, since $b\natural'$, the 5th of Em7, is a good melodic continuation from bar one. The II – V phrase (a) outlines the resolution 7th of Em7 to 3rd of A7. The last four notes of the phrase are a fragment of a descending D minor (harmonic) scale; this leads logically to the choice of the next II – V phrase (b), which commences on the 3rd of Dm7. The upwards movement of the new phrase also balances the downwards movement of the preceding bar.

(ii)   Bar four (phrase c) falls back on the simple device of transposing the previous bar down a tone. So long as it is not overdone, such exact transposition of II – V ideas can be effective.

(iii)   Bars five to seven contain basically only one idea (bar 5) which is developed by rhythmic variation together with adaptation and transposition. The simple major phrase on B♭Δ is adapted to fit the next bar (B♭m7 E♭7) by flattening the 3rd, and rhythmically varied by including three syncopations instead of one. This phrase (d) is followed by phrase (e) on Am7 D7, which is, except for one note, an exact transposition of phrase (d) but without syncopation.

(iv)   Bar eight contrasts the previous three bars (all based on the same idea), with a new II – V phrase (f). But continuity is preserved by the fact that this phrase, like phrases (d) and (e), starts on the 5th of its II chord (A♭m7).

(v)   Bars nine to twelve contain a two-bar II – V phrase (in contrast to the one-bar II – Vs of the first eight bars), which leads to a sustained note over the turnaround of the last two bars.

Many words have just been used to describe the reasons for choosing the phrases of a particular, short improvisation—reasons which, in fact, a soloist would hardly be aware of at the moment of improvising. But, to arrive at the stage where it is possible to create a logical solo without consciously reflecting on each phrase, a jazz musician will have spent many hours of thinking about and practising individual phrases, ways of varying them, and connecting them up to form continuous lines. Detailed analysis of existing solos is essential practice for any improviser.

Improvisation 'works' by calling on a stock of premeditated (practised) ideas and the choice of an appropriate phrase at a particular point is dictated by the need for melodic continuity, a balance of melodic direction, and rhythmic variety.

How to Practise

How do you practise producing an infinite number of improvisations on, for example, the round-the-clock sequence? Try building a new improvisation under the three types of phrase revealed by the analysis above:

MAJOR TONIC CENTRE PHRASES

TWO-BAR II – V PHRASES

ONE-BAR II – V PHRASES

(i)   File each phrase of the sample solo (example 87) mentally under its appropriate heading, and then analyse it in terms of the chord or chords beneath it. For example:

Bar: 1
Heading: major tonic centre phrase
Analysis:

(ii)   Transpose each phrase under a particular heading to the same chord(s) for comparison. For example, compare these one-bar II – V phrases from the sample solo, all transposed over Dm7–G7:

81

Ex. 89

(iii) Transpose each phrase of the sample solo (example 87) to every key. Major tonic centre phrases should be transposed on a bass moving up and down the chromatic scale a step at a time, and also around the cycle of 4ths; II – V phrases should be transposed on a bass of 'II – Vs in tones' (example 85) or 'chromatic II – Vs' (example 86) over one or two bars, according to phrase-length:

(iv) Interchange any phrase in the solo with another of the same heading. For example, bars 1 and 5 are both major tonic centre phrases and can be interchanged over the appropriate chord. (You will already have played the transposition in exercise (iii).) The solo has five different one-bar II – V phrases which can be interchanged with each other.

The practical results of developing the ability to transpose and interchange phrases amount to more than being able to reshuffle a few ideas to make up a 'new' solo. Each phrase that you use over a particular chord or movement creates its own problem of continuity, leading to fresh connections and adjustments of ideas.

The benefits of being able to transpose ideas are not confined to improvising on one particular sequence. If a II – V phrase has been learnt in twelve keys, it can be used over any II – V movement in any tune and key.

The melodic ideas used to illustrate this method of practice are drawn from a sample solo, but you should develop your own stock of ideas to practise.

Tritone Substitutions

Round-the-clock changes may be varied, like the standard blues, with tritone substitutions for II – V progressions (see chapter 5) at key points, such as bars four and ten:

FΔ	Em7 A7	Dm7 G7	4 Cm7 F7 (F♯m7 B7)
B♭Δ	B♭m7 E♭7	Am7 D7	A♭m7 D♭7
Gm7	10 Gm7 C7 (D♭m7 G♭7)	FΔ D7	Gm7 C7

These tritone II – Vs can be 'run' by suitably transposing a II – V phrase from existing stock. But there is a special skill in negotiating tritone II – Vs so that the chosen phrase resolves naturally. How can you continue the following tritone II – V phrase in bar four so that it resolves onto B♭Δ?

Ex. 90

Improvising on Turnarounds

One way to play over the turnaround is to ignore the changes and simply play in the key of the piece. A phrase such as

Ex. 91

will suit the turnaround very well—for the same reason that blues-scale phrases suit the same chords elsewhere in a blues sequence (see chapter 11, page 73). A diatonic rather than a blues-scale phrase will also serve, perhaps with some chromatic added notes:

Ex. 92

The other way to play over a turnaround is to run its changes:

Ex. 93

Turnarounds are not only a feature of any blues but they form the endings of eight-bar sections of many standard jazz numbers.

Variations on the Turnaround

The four chords of the turnaround (e.g. in the key of F) can be altered in a number of ways. Each chord may be a flat 7th:

F7 D7	G7 C7
I7 VI7	II7 V7

or

A7 D7	G7 C7
III7 VI7	II7 V7

These 'straight 7th' turnarounds can be further altered by using tritone substitutes for the 2nd and 4th chords:

F7 A♭7	G7 G♭7
I7 ♭III7	II7 ♭II7

or

A7 A♭7	G7 G♭7
III7 ♭III7	II7 ♭II7

If tritone substitutes are used for the first and third chord, you will play:

Eb7 D7	Db7 C7
bVII7 VI7	bVI7 V7

This list does not exhaust the possibilities. Finally, the standard 'altered' turnaround, which does not quite correspond to any of the above, is this:

FΔ Ab7	DbΔ Gb7b5
IΔ bIII7	bVIΔ bII7

Compared to the original turnaround of F7 – D7 | Gm7 – C7 ‖, Ab7 and Gb7 are the tritone substitutions of D7 and C7, but DbΔ is not an exact tritone substitute for Gm7. This standard 'altered' turnaround is effective as it contains a vivid modulation from F to Db and, by using DbΔ (instead of Dbm7) and the flat 5th in Gb, all four chords are linked by one common note (C).

85

13 AABA FORM: B♭

Moving to the next key in the cycle after C and F, the most widely-used sequence is based on the changes typified by George Gershwin's *I got rhythm*. The rhythm changes (as they are commonly called) are the archetypal thirty-two bar AABA song form.

There are four eight-bar sections—AABA—in which the ⸢A⸣ sections are almost identical and the contrasting ⸢B⸣ section is the 'middle eight'. The *I got rhythm* changes are:

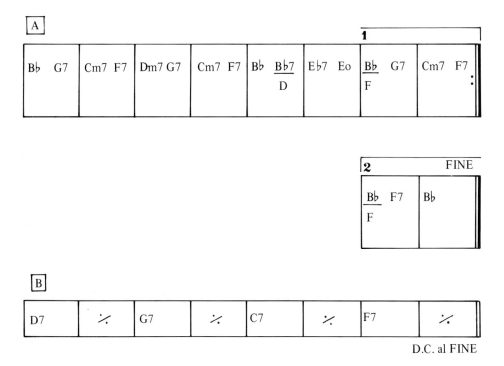

Compare these rhythm-changes in B♭ with a 'modern' twelve-bar blues in the same key:

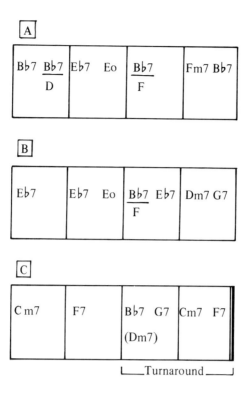

The two-bar turnaround of the blues, repeated, becomes the first four of *I got rhythm* (first on chord I, then on III); the first two bars of the blues are bars five and six; the blues turnaround again provides bars seven and eight. If you know your blues changes, there is no problem with the A sections of *I got rhythm*.

This leaves B the middle eight which is a straightforward sequence of four flat 7th chords with a bass following the cycle of fourths, from III (D7) to V (F7), each lasting two bars.

Here is a sample solo over the first eight bars of the rhythm changes:

Ex. 94

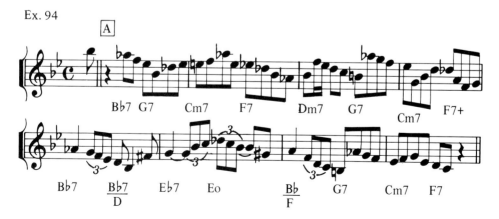

87

For the middle eight, the possibilities are endless but to start with 'borrow' or make up a phrase for the first two bars of D7 such as:

Ex. 95

and then transpose this to fit the next three chords (G7, C7, F7). This is a good way to practise, but for a 'real' solo, three transpositions of one idea are probably a bit unimaginative. With even one alternate phrase, the number of routes through the middle eight increases to four. Here is a possible alternate phrase for the second two bars:

Ex. 96

If bars one and two of the middle eight are thought of as phrase *a* and bars three and four as phrase *b*, the permutations available for the whole eight are:

B *a b a b*
B *b a b a*
B *a b b a*
B *b a a b*

If each bar is thought of as a phrase in itself (*a b c d* = bars 1, 2, 3 and 4) the permutations over the whole eight bars are 24 ('factorial 4').

Variations: A Sections

All the turnaround variations listed at the end of the previous chapter can be used in the A sections of *I got rhythm* changes, together with these:

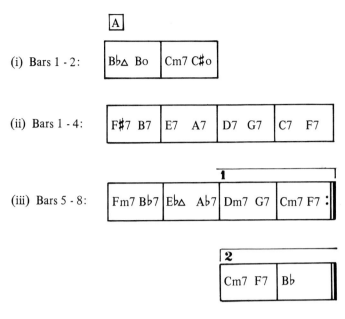

(i) Bars 1 - 2:

Bb△ Bo	Cm7 C♯o

(ii) Bars 1 - 4:

F♯7 B7	E7 A7	D7 G7	C7 F7

1

(iii) Bars 5 - 8:

Fm7 Bb7	Eb△ Ab7	Dm7 G7	Cm7 F7 :‖

2

Cm7 F7	Bb

The soloist can employ any of these variations and the rhythm section (piano/guitar, bass) should be able to follow: if the rhythm section decide by prior arrangement (or to challenge the soloist!) on any of these variations, the soloist can over-ride them by playing on the basic chords. The only exception, which no ear can follow quickly without prior agreement, is variation (ii) beginning on F♯7; this variation, though very effective, must be pre-arranged.

Variations: Middle Eight B

One common variation is to make each two-bar chord into a II – V movement by replacing the first bar with the minor 7th chord a fifth above the original chord:

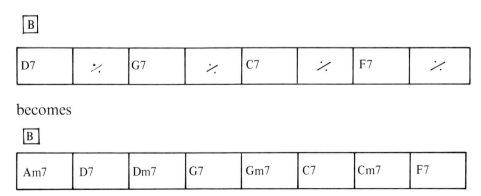

B

D7	∕.	G7	∕.	C7	∕.	F7	∕.

becomes

B

Am7	D7	Dm7	G7	Gm7	C7	Cm7	F7

89

This makes four two-bar II – Vs following the cycle of 4ths and you can then think of the middle eight as four two-bar II – Vs instead of four phrases on two-bar chords. In this way, a typical II – V phrase from bars nine and ten of a twelve-bar blues might be transposed to the first two bars of an *I got rhythm* middle eight:

Ex. 97

To learn another variation, think of G7, C7 and F7 (bars 3, 5 and 7 of the middle eight) as temporary dominant 7ths of new keys and follow them by half-bar II – Vs in the 'new' key:

B									
Am7	D7	G7	Dm7 G7	C7	Gm7 C7	F7	Cm7 F7
	to C:	V	II V	I			
		to F:	V		II V	I	
			to B♭:			V	II V

to A :
(last eight)

Here is a possible middle-eight solo on the above variations:

Ex. 98

90

This solo also works over the basic middle-eight changes. You may now have discovered that it is always possible to play over one *or* two bars of a V chord as if it were a II – V movement. It is equally possible to play over any II – V movement as if it were simply a V chord.

A final variation to the middle eight may use tritone substitutes for alternate chords:

B

D7	∕.	G7 Db7	∕. ∕.	C7	∕.	F7 B7	∕. ∕.

or

D7 Ab7	∕. ∕.	G7	∕.	C7 F#7	∕. ∕.	F7	∕.

In both cases, the result is a sequence of 7ths descending chromatically rather than following the cycle of 4ths.

Exercises

(i)   Complete the empty bars of the following variation of the *I got rhythm* middle eight with II – V tritone substitutions for the preceding bars:

B

Am7 D7	? ?	Dm7 G7	? ?	Gm7 C7	? ?	Cm7 F7	? ?

(ii)   Take any one-bar II – V phrase and transpose it through the above sequence.

91

14 EXPANDING YOUR REPERTOIRE

The harmonic and melodic vocabulary developed by studying the twelve-bar blues and thirty-two-bar *I got rhythm* changes equips you to deal with most of the standard repertoire of jazz. Each new number you learn will be found to include harmonic movements you have already met in the blues, rhythm changes or both.

Honeysuckle Rose in F

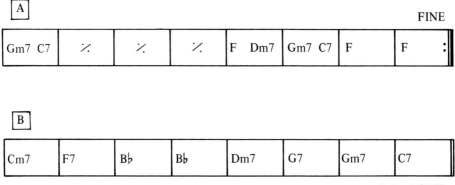

These changes are a simplified version of those actually played by Fats Waller in his original solo recording of his famous tune. The form of *Honeysuckle Rose*—thirty-two bars, AABA—is exactly the same as that of *I got rhythm*, and the basic changes are even more straightforward.

Scrapple from the Apple in F

If you know the *I got rhythm* and *Honeysuckle Rose* changes (both easy to memorise) and can improvise on both, it should be easy to learn the changes to the well-known Charlie Parker tune *Scrapple from the Apple*, which consist of the [A] sections of *Honeysuckle Rose* (slightly rejigged) and the [B] section of *I got rhythm*. The theme for *Scrapple* should be learned from the recording. These are the changes:

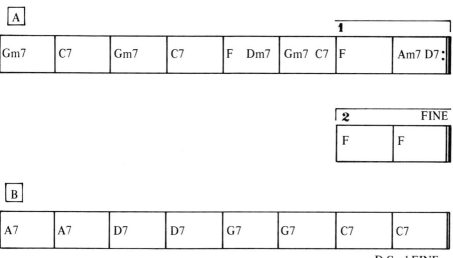

The [A] section changes are not only those of *Honeysuckle Rose*, but may also be memorised by thinking of the blues in F and *I got rhythm*: bars one to two and three to four are two-bar II – Vs, corresponding to bars nine and ten of a blues in F; bars five and six, a two-bar turnaround in F, correspond to the first two bars of *I got rhythm* (with one difference, VIm7 instead of VI7); and bars seven and eight are a turnaround leading back to II, corresponding to bars seven and eight of a blues in F.

Here is a sample improvisation for the first eight on these changes:

Complete a chorus by improvising a second eight, a middle eight and last eight on the changes of *Scrapple from the Apple* ([A1], [B], [A]).

Confirmation

This is one of the most challenging of Charlie Parker's compositions. If at all possible, this should be learned from the recording (1963 quartet version); if this is too difficult, the transcription in the Parker Omnibook (Atlantic Music Corporation, New York) may be used. Here are the changes:.

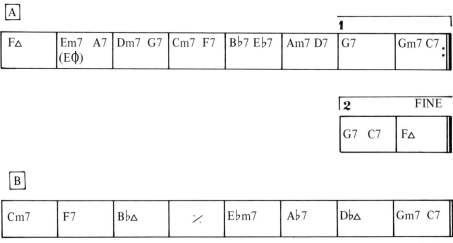

Here is an improvisation on the first eight of *Confirmation* (the first four bars are 'borrowed' from the sample round-the-clock blues solo on page 79 to show how your own ideas can be transferred from number to number):

Ex. 100

Complete the chorus by improvising second, middle and last eights on the *Confirmation* changes.

Themes for Improvisation

Lastly, as playing the blues and *I got rhythm* changes will figure large in your improvising, here is a list of useful themes or 'heads' for these two basic jazz forms. Unless otherwise noted, the definitive recordings of these titles are by the composers. First, the blues:

Title	Usual key	Composer/performer
Blue Monk	B♭	Thelonious Monk
Straight No Chaser	F	Thelonious Monk (recorded by Miles Davis)
Bag's Groove	F	Milt Jackson (recorded by Miles Davis)
Royal Roost Blues (*aka* Tenor Madness)	F or B♭	Kenny Dorham (recorded by Sonny Rollins and John Coltrane)
Now's the time	F	Charlie Parker
Billie's Bounce	F	Charlie Parker
Au Privave	F	Charlie Parker
Blues for Alice	F (round the clock)	Charlie Parker
Sandu	E♭	Clifford Brown
Blue 'n' Boogie	B♭	Dizzy Gillespie (recorded by Miles Davis)
Walkin'	F	Richard Carpenter (recorded by Miles Davis)
Vierd Blues (*aka* Trane's Blues)	B♭	Miles Davis
Blues by Five	F	Miles Davis
Sonnymoon for Two	B♭	Sonny Rollins
Cousin Mary	A♭	John Coltrane
Blue Trane	E♭	John Coltrane
Some Other Blues	F	John Coltrane

The tune of *I got rhythm* is seldom used as a theme itself. Instead, most musicians today prefer to use one of the many themes composed by the 'greats' to the rhythm changes. Early 'rhythm-change' themes such as Lester Young's *Lester Leaps In* are simple riffs dating from the 1930s. Themes of the be-bop period (early 1940s to early 1950s) are melodically and rhythmically more complex. They are really written-out improvisations and, as such, make excellent study material. Try to memorise at least two or three of these rhythm-change themes by ear from the recordings which are readily available.

Title	Key	Composer/performer
Lester Leaps in	B♭	Lester Young
Moose the Mooche	B♭	Charlie Parker
Anthropology	B♭	Dizzy Gillespie/Charlie Parker
Dexterity	B♭	Charlie Parker
Oleo	B♭	Sonny Rollins (recorded by Miles Davis with Rollins; and also with John Coltrane)
Chasing the Bird	F	Charlie Parker
The Theme (*aka* Miles's Theme)	B♭	Miles Davis

Acknowledgment

The quotation in the Introduction is reprinted from *The Study of Counterpoint* (1725) by Johann Joseph Fux, translated and edited by Alfred Mann, by permission of W. W. Norton and Co. Inc. Copyright © 1965, 1943 by W. W. Norton and Co. Inc. Copyright renewed 1971 by Alfred Mann.